GREATEST MY TEST

CHALLENGE

Reclaiming My Life After My Brain Hemorrhage

FRANK KIENAST

BALBOA
PRESS
A DIVISION OF HAY HOUSE

Balboa Press books may be ordered through booksellers or by contacting:

Balboa Press
A Division of Hay House
1663 Liberty Drive
Bloomington, IN 47403
www.balboapress.com
1 (877) 407-4847

Because of the dynamic nature of the Internet, any web addresses or links contained in this book may have changed since publication and may no longer be valid. The views expressed in this work are solely those of the author and do not necessarily reflect the views of the publisher, and the publisher hereby disclaims any responsibility for them.

The author of this book does not dispense medical advice or prescribe the use of any technique as a form of treatment for physical, emotional, or medical problems without the advice of a physician, either directly or indirectly. The intent of the author is only to offer information of a general nature to help you in your quest for emotional and spiritual well-being. In the event you use any of the information in this book for yourself, which is your constitutional right, the author and the publisher assume no responsibility for your actions.

Any people depicted in stock imagery provided by Thinkstock are models, and such images are being used for illustrative purposes only. Certain stock imagery © Thinkstock.

Print information available on the last page.

ISBN: 978-1-5043-3017-6 (sc)
ISBN: 978-1-5043-3018-3 (e)

Balboa Press rev. date: 4/7/2015

INTRODUCTION

According to the American Stroke Association, between 3 and 5 million people in the United States have or will develop a ticking time bomb known as a cerebral aneurysm. Yet most of these aneurysms produce no symptoms. Only a few percent eventually bleed. Since the surgery to remove a brain aneurysm carries a higher risk than the risk of an eventual bleed, even people who are determined to have a brain aneurysm are seldom treated[1]

Most people have never had an MRI scan of their brain, so they may have a cerebral aneurysm without even knowing it. Yet I actually knew I had a cerebral aneurysm. I didn't pay any attention, but I knew it.

Way back in 1990, I was diagnosed with severe hypothyroidism. I had been experiencing many of

---

[1]   Mayo Clinic, "Diseases and Conditions: Brain Aneurysm: Basics", http://www.mayoclinic.org/diseases-conditions/brain-aneurysm/basics/definition/con-20028457.

the symptoms for several years – cold extremities, intolerance to cold, low energy, slow reflexes and thinking. I had been to a doctor and specifically had my thyroid tested several years earlier, but was told that my thyroid levels were within the normal range at that time. By late 1990, though, I knew something was wrong. I felt like I was "in a fog" much of the time, and could not concentrate. I had a low body temperature and a lack of energy. In December 1990, extensive testing revealed a severe case of hypothyroidism. I would need to take synthetic thyroid hormone for the rest of my life, but this would eventually resolve my symptoms.

Yet when I started the thyroid hormone, I instead developed severe new symptoms. I could not sleep at all many nights. My heart was constantly pounding. I felt so on edge that I couldn't concentrate even enough to read at times. I was sure something more serious was wrong – perhaps a brain tumor I thought since my thinking was so drastically affected. My endocrinologist did not think there was anything wrong. While she admitted that my symptoms were extreme, she still attributed them to adjustment to the thyroid hormone. Having normal thyroid hormones was a shock to my body since I had been deficient for years. She referred me to a psychiatrist for help with adjusting to and dealing with the symptoms. But I was not convinced. I was sure that something had to be wrong inside my brain. I asked if there was a medical test that could be done to detect a "brain tumor or other problem in the brain". I was told that yes, I could have an MRI scan. Even though it was highly unlikely that I had a brain tumor, my doctor was willing to schedule an MRI if it would give me peace of mind.

I had the MRI on December 27, 1990. I remember the doctor telling me the results. He said "There was an abnormality detected". He then described an abnormality that I now know is a cerebral aneurysm. As soon as I heard him say I had an abnormality, I felt vindicated. "See, I knew there was something wrong up there.", I said. The doctor replied, "Oh, that's not causing you any problems now!" "You mean it's not causing my insomnia and anxiety and inability to concentrate?", I asked. "No, it's not presently causing any problems whatsoever." "Then is it serious? Is it something I need to be concerned with?" He said something to the effect of "maybe, maybe not". Its been many years so I don't remember the details of what he said, I'm pretty sure he told the the statistics about the majority of brain aneurysms not rupturing, and the fact that they are not normally treated. Maybe he mentioned that was perhaps something to possibly monitor with another scan many years later. But it didn't matter. I did not have a brain tumor, or anything to worry about at the time.

I went on to make a complete recovery over the next two months. With help from medicines for anxiety and depression, I was soon my old self, doing everything I had done before. In fact, I was doing better than before, because my thyroid problem was now corrected. The psychiatric medicines were discontinued uneventfully over the coming months. I continued to take the synthetic thyroid hormone from then on, with occasional adjustments in amount based on lab tests.

I never thought about the "abnormality" in my brain again in the coming years. I never made any connection to the fact that my mother had almost died from a brain aneurysm that happened when she was 39 years old.

Though I was only five years old at the time, I vividly remember my mother collapsing from a ruptured brain aneurysm back in February of 1970. My mother was a Sunday School teacher at my church, and I was in her class. She was holding up a Bible bank and talking about it to the class. Suddenly the bank flew out of her hands and went bouncing across the room, while she fell forward to the floor with a loud thud. For many weeks after that, I remember my father telling me he didn't know if my mom would live or die. I remember he would see her in the intensive care room of the hospital, and I would have to wait outside.

Treatment for ruptured brain aneurysms was pretty primitive at the time. The doctors made a large incision in her neck, and somehow closed off the artery that was bleeding. This left her with a permanent large scar. Even once home, it would require many months of home nursing before my mother was able to even care for herself, much less my father and me. Although I was too young to be able to make a comparison, my father tells me that my mother never completely regained her old personality or the zest for living that she possessed prior to the ruptured aneurysm. But that was in 1970. Medicine has advanced greatly since then.

More than 40 years later, my life would also be turned upside down by a ruptured brain aneurysm very similar to the one my mother had. The genetic component of brain aneurysms is not understood in detail. Most brain aneurysms, in fact, are not hereditary. They are caused by life style. High blood pressure, excessive smoking, drinking, or use of stimulant drugs such as cocaine and amphetamines are the biggest risks for causing brain aneurysms. Yet I had none of these risk factors. So then why did I have a brain aneurysm? I found out a year later that I have a bicuspid aortic valve (BAV). See the chapter "The Aortic Valve is Bicuspid" for details). This is a congenital (birth) defect. As it turns out, this is not only a disorder of the heart, but also affects the entire circulatory system of the body. People born with BAV are at ten times the normal risk of having a brain aneurysm[2].

In this book, I will describe how my life was changed by my ruptured brain aneurysm that occurred on April 26, 2013. I will describe the specific events associated with the aneurysm as they occurred and the emotions I experienced during the events. Life threw many obstacles in my path as I worked to recover from the

---

[2] Neurology, American Academy of Neurology, April 4, 2010, As reported by Science Daily, http://www.sciencedaily.com/releases/2010/05/100503161227.htm.

aneurysm and return to a normal, productive live. I will describe the major obstacles I faced and how I was ultimately able to overcome each one. I hope my story will serve as an inspiration to others facing recovery from a brain aneurysm or other serious illness or adversity.

Why did I write this book? The main reason was for myself. I needed to come to terms with the things that had happened to me. I really needed to get things "off my chest", so to speak. Many brain aneurysm survivors are lucky enough to have a caregiver who can serve as a close confident. This might be a spouse, relative, or close friend. I did not have any such outlets, and I did not feel comfortable bending the ear of any friends to constantly talk about my condition. Some of the books I read on integrating traumatic experience recommended writing a journal in this case.

I also realized that I had been helped quite a bit when I was working to overcome my iatrogenic benzodiazepine addiction (see the chapter "Addicted to Klonopin") by reading a book by someone else who had recovered from the same situation. As an engineer by training, I know I have a very logical (sometimes to a fault) approach to handling things that happen to me. I thought therefore that my logical approach to overcoming the many issues I recovered during my recovery might be able to help others reason through things as well.

Finally, any and all proceeds from sales of this book will go towards will be given to the Brain Aneurysm

Foundation (www.bafound.org), the nation's premier nonprofit organization solely dedicated to providing critical awareness, education, support and research funding to reduce the incidence of brain aneurysm ruptures. Even if the proceeds are only a few dollars, at least I can feel I did a a little something more than I would have had I just stuck to writing a journal.

This is a pretty specialized book. It is not meant to be the next great novel or thriller. It is likely to seem boring at best, and sound like endless complaining at worst, to someone who has not been affected a brain aneurysm or other serious illness. The situations and problems I faced in recovery may in fact seem pretty trivial. And they probably mostly are, to someone in good health. Yet readers who themselves have experienced a brain aneurysm, other type of stroke, or traumatic head injury will know exactly where I am coming from in my descriptions. As will the caregivers for such victims.

I'm a fairly "weird" person. I've been called, at various times, a geek, a loaner, a mad scientist, and probably other things that I should not mention here. I have weird hobbies, such as storm chasing. I don't try to flaunt my "weirdness" in this book, but I don't try to hide it, and it is apparent in my descriptions of day-to-day activities. I am also a Christian. I don't make apologies for referring to my faith, church life, etc. But nor do I try to "convert" the reader to my beliefs. On the contrary, I am comfortable talking about how these events in my life tested my faith, and how some aspects of religious faith and practice, though good in intent, actually served to make things worse for me.

The technical term for my medical event, and what is shown on my hospital papers, is "subarachnoid hemorrhage". It literally means a hemorrhage (bleeding) in the area between the brain and the scull. This is considered a type of stroke. For the sake of sounding less technical and for variety as I refer to this frequently, I will use several terms interchangeably to refer to this condition. These terms include (among others) "subarachnoid hemorrhage", "brain aneurysm", "ruptured brain aneurysm", "brain hemorrhage", "homorrhagic stroke", "bleed in the brain" and "stroke".

At several points in this book, I refer to co-workers, church members, and friends who I interacted with. I have changed their names in this book to ensure their privacy. In addition, I refer to several things that happened to other caregivers in the Christian Care and Support ministry I am a part of at my church. To protect the confidentiality of these people, I have made significant changes to the cases, and in some instances have created composites of events happening to several different people. Rest assured though that I have not exaggerated or made significant conceptual changes to these events.

I began writing this book shortly after my one-year followup surgery in April, 2014. As I began writing, the chapter titles I wanted to include came to me spontaneously early on. It was then a matter of filling in these chapters over the next 8 months or so. Once I completed the draft, I then went back and revised each chapter to add references, and in some cases to clarify things and improve the flow.

Thank you for reading this book. I hope it helps you in some way.

Frank Kienast
December, 2014

A FORESHADOWING

According to the Brain Aneurysm foundation, the symptoms of a bleed in the brain include "Sudden severe headache, the worst headache of your life". I never had this symptom. Even on the night of my brain hemorrhage, I had no headache. Yet I did have an unusually large number of headaches in the the two months preceding April 26, 2013.

I like to take as little medicine as possible. When I do need to take something, say for a headache or a cold, I record it on my calendar. According to my 2013 calendar, I took aspirin for headache symptoms six times in March and twice in April. This is a very high number for me. Normally, I might get a headache and take aspirin once or twice in a month. For example, in both January and February, I took aspirin once for a headache. After I got out of the hospital from my surgery, I only took medicine for headache a total of 8 times over the following 7 months. But in March and April, I was having a lot of headaches. None were severe, and I attributed them to their normal cause (stress). And perhaps there is no connection between the headaches and the aneurysm. But for me, this was a high frequency of headaches.

Since early childhood, I have been fascinated by storms and by weather in general. In 2010, I saw my first tornado on a storm chasing tour. I went on another storm chasing tour in 2012, but I found that tour stressful due to the long drive times. We drove of 3500 miles in the course of a one-week tour. We were looking for the biggest storms – that could potentially produce tornadoes. I was interested in thunderstorms of all types – not just those that produce tornadoes. Living in the Buffalo, NY area, one does not get to see much in the way of thunderstorms. Besides being located pretty far to the north, Lake Erie prevents thunderstorms from forming in the immediate Buffalo area during most of the summer. I missed seeing the big thunderstorms I saw during my childhood in southeastern Virginia and the six years I lived in Indiana. So late in 2012, I got to thinking to myself. Why don't I live someplace not too far away that does get a lot of thunderstorms, just for a few months. I could probably do that for the cost of airfare and a week-long tornado chase tour. That way I would be able to chase the storms I was interested in, without having to be on the road so much since I would be satisfied with less severe storms and would not have to drive as far to chase.

So by early 2013, I was getting all set for a summer of living remotely and chasing storms. I was fortunate that the work I do (as a software developer) allows me to

2

work remotely when necessary. Indeed, several other employees in my department were working remotely, two of them permanently. My boss approved me working remotely for the summer without needing to give it much consideration. I settled on Columbus, Ohio as the location where I would look for a temporary place to live. This was close enough that I could easily get back to Buffalo in one day if an emergency came up at work. That area received plenty of storms. In addition, it was close enough to states where old friends lived (Indiana, West Virginia, and Virginia) that I would also likely be able to see my friends in person for the first time in years on weekend trips. I began preparing. I looked at apartments in Columbus that offered a short-term lease and would allow my pet cat. Being an electronics geek, I had built and bought a variety of lightning detectors that would alert me to and allow me to track storms by February.

On Saturday April 6, I drove to Columbus to view several apartments and make my decision. I had been looking forward to that date for months. Yet I found myself getting very stressed out. Work had been hectic the previous week, with many deadlines and the need to get up hours early for implementations on a couple of days. I really needed a weekend to relax, not undertake more stressful activities. But the time had finally arrived for me to finalize my summer plans.

As it turned out, the weekend did nothing but add to my stress. All of the apartments I visited except for one had numerous fees not disclosed online. Such as

$800 non-refundable pet fees and various surcharges in addition to the higher rates charged for short-term rental. The one place that had a somewhat reasonable price was in a location where a bunch of road work was just starting. Already dealing with traffic jams caused by the current rapid growth and associated construction in downtown Buffalo, I wasn't interested in paying a lot of money for a place where the traffic problems would be even worse. And I was not convinced that the neighborhood there would be quiet enough for me to work productively.

So when I returned to Buffalo late Sunday, I was not ready for another week of work. I needed time to relax and figure out what I was going to do. As it turned out, I had headaches on both Monday and Tuesday. But work would not wait. Eventually, I reluctantly decided that I would remain in Buffalo for the summer. When storms were likely, I would drive to places to the south – in Pennsylvania and Ohio – the day before. I would stay at a motel and work from there. This would be more cost effective than renting an apartment for summer, and would allow me to chase in a wider area.

Besides the stress, headaches, and bad luck locating an apartment, there was other foreshadowing of the trouble I would soon be facing with my brain aneurysm.

One morning early in April, I arrived at work and had an itch in my nose. Not thinking anything of it, I scratched it as I got out of my car. As I closed my car door, I was shocked to see drops of blood dripping from my nose. I squeezed my nose and quickly made my way to the restroom inside my work building, where I was able to stop the bleeding after about ten minutes. I was shocked that this had happened. While I was plagued with nose bleeds as a child, they had never been a problem for me since adulthood. To this day, I still wonder if there is any connection between this unusual bleeding, and the bleeding that would occur in my brain several weeks later. And I think there might be. The previous summer, my doctor started me on a statin drug. This was based on my age (48), and the fact that my "good" cholesterol is genetically low. While this preventative measure may well reduce the risk of a heart attack or (non-hemorrhagic) stroke, I have since learned that statins thin the blood and can actually increase the chances for a hemorrhagic stroke. I had had a brain aneurysm for many years, but it had never ruptured. Perhaps the blood-thinning effects of the statin were what caused the aneurysm to bleed.

I was scheduled to visit my elderly father in Virginia beginning on May 1. Since he does not have internet access, I decided to buy a wireless internet hub to allow me to maintain internet connectivity during my visit. I ordered this online, and it arrived on April 16th. On April 16th, I was working from home due to having to be online for work at 5:30AM for an implementation. The package arrived by noon, so at lunchtime I was was busy testing out the new device. But I couldn't get it to work. Investigation revealed that is was missing a SIM card. A SIM card is used to uniquely identify the device for billing purposes. It was supposed to have been included in the package, but it was not. So I would either need to ship the package back and wait, or find a local store that could help me. I contacted the support number and was told that there was in fact a local store that could supply me with the needed SIM card. Since I would already have worked well beyond the normal 8-hour workday by late afternoon, I decided I would drive to the store around 3PM and get the problem taken care of.

I finished my work for the day and set out for the store. It was a club store, with the phone service center located within. I am not a member of the club, but was allowed inside once I explained that I was visiting the service center located within the store. It was a long process to get everything straightened out and working, but an hour or so later, I was all set and ready to go home.

By this point, it was probably well past 4PM, and many people were out doing errands after work. Traffic was heavy. Since I had many "Type A" personality characteristics and tended to get quite impatient with delays, I almost never went out at that time of day. Likewise, I have never been inside the shopping center where the phone repair center was located before, preferring to shop mostly online. I remember waiting, and waiting, for the light at the exit from the shopping center to turn green so I could get on my way. It seems I must have sat there five or ten minutes. Finally, the light changed. The person ahead of me turned left, which I also needed to do. In my distraction and unfamiliarity with the intersection, I didn't realize that there was no left turn signal, and that there there was also another shopping center across the street that had also gotten a green light. As I was crossing the road doing my left turn, I saw another car coming out of the shopping center across the street, headed directly for the side of my car. Somehow I managed to steer around that car and the car right behind it, to the sound of several horns blasting. I came out of the situation unscathed physically, but with a rapidly pounding heart and full of adrenaline.

That I had had such a close call would be unnerving under any circumstances. But I was already very stressed out by recent events and having to be up early that day for a work implementation. The fact that I had made such an elementary driving mistake when I was preparing for a summer involving thousands of miles of driving for storm chasing made it all the more discouraging. I returned home to ponder the implications.

There was to be one more warning prior to the rupture of my brain aneurysm on April 26th. On Sunday April 21st, early church service had just let out. As I prepared to go downstairs to teach Sunday School, I experienced sort of a panic attack. It was like I suddenly experienced a big shot of adrenaline. My heart sped up, I got a sinking feeling in my stomach, and my mouth became dry. I attributed this to stress. I knew I was still under a tremendous amount of stress. In the past, I have occasionally experienced similar symptoms, often when relaxing while under stress. I told myself "Wow, I must be

ONE AND ONLY STORM CHASE

After my unsuccessful attempt to find a place to live in "storm country" for the summer, I let my boss know that I would not, in fact, be working remotely for most of the original period I had indicated (early June through mid-August). Instead, I would be staying in Buffalo most of the time. However, when storms were likely, I would be driving to the area of the storms and working remotely from a motel for a couple of days each time.

On the evening of April 9, a few weak thunderstorms developed not far from where I live in Orchard Park. Although lightning amounts were not particularly impressive, the strikes were enough to allow me to do an initial calibration on several lightning detectors I had purchased and one I had built. As the storm approached, I scrambled to correlate distances shown by radar and online lightning strike data to distances being estimated by my detectors. By the time the storm was over, I was satisfied that I had made been able to do a fairly good initial calibration of all the detectors.

My alarm clock woke me for work on Thursday morning (April 10). I hit the snooze button. As I laid there awake in the darkness, I saw what appeared to be a flashing light dimly in the room. I assumed it must be a tow truck or similar vehicle outside the window. Then I glanced over to one of the lightning detectors, which was mounted on a bedroom wall. I saw that one of the LEDs on the detector was flashing. I got up and checked weather radar data online. Sure enough, there was a week storm about 30 miles to the south. The front that had produced the storm the previous evening was now stationary just south of the area. It looked like there might be a chance of more storms in the local area later in the day (depending on the exact position of the front). But areas just a bit to the south – in western Pennsylvania – were likely to see significant storms.

When I got to work, I checked the radar again. Sure enough, significant storms were already developing over Ohio and moving east. As I continued to check the radar from time to time, I saw the storms intensifying. I realized that these storms would likely reach western Pennsylvania during the afternoon. Watching the storms on radar, I was having difficulty staying focused on my work. I wished it was time to chase now. But then I thought – well why not? These storms might not be real impressive by June standards, but if I were to chase now it would give me practice for later chases. And I could probably get back home the same evening, without having to stay anyplace or work remotely. It would just be a question of if I could get approval from my boss.

My boss was continually in meetings, so I could not get in to see him and ask if I could take the rest of the day off for chasing. I continued my work. I continued checking the radar from time to time. And the storms continued developing. Finally, late in the morning, I was able to catch my boss. The conversation went something like this: "Pedro, looks like there are some storms developing to the south of here. I would like to chase these, if that's possible, today. Everything is complete and all set for tomorrow's early morning implementation, and I will still be available for that." "So, does that mean you are going to go chasing and be killed by a tornado?" "No, of course not. There are not likely to be any tornadoes. But there are some decent storms headed for western Pennsylvania, and I would like to chase them. Would it be okay for me to take a half day of vacation time today so I can chase them?" "Well, I certainly don't want anything happening to you. There's plenty of work that we need you on this week." "Nothing is going to happen to me. I'm just going to drive south, video tape the storms, and then come back this evening. I'll use a half day of vacation time for this. Is that okay?" "If you want to take the rest of the day off, it's fine with me." "Thanks, Pedro!"

I left work and headed southwest on Interstate 90. Skies were dull overcast, and the outdoor thermometer in my car showed a temperature in the low 40's as I drove. I drove through some heavy rain showers shortly after crossing the Pennsylvania border. Temperatures, though, were still only in the mid-40s. I needed to get south of the front.

I stopped and checked weather radar using the RadarScope app on my phone. The storms were still on their way, and in fact they were moving faster than I expected. It looked like someplace just north of Pittsburgh would be an ideal target chase location. However, it would be close if I could get there in time. If not, however, other storms looked to pass a bit further north as well. I headed south in Interstate 79.

As I continued to drive south, temperatures warmed well into the 50's. The sky changed from being a dull overcast to having summer-looking cumulus clouds. I drove through heavy rain showers in places. As I reached a point about 40 miles north of Pittsburgh, the main storm was upon me. I found an exit and pulled off to film the storm. There was lightning, but the storm was not particularly impressive.

There was another strong storm, but it was south and west of Pittsburgh. I debated chasing after it. But since it would not arrive for a couple of hours, and this would put me ever further from home, I was not sure if it was worth it. Then I checked to the north and saw a line of storms developing. It would be going through Erie, PA in a couple of hours. I could easily get there in time. And I would be be back closer to home. So I turned around and began heading north on Interstate 79.

Skies were a dull overcast and the temperature down in the 40s again as I approached Erie. From these conditions, it seemed hard to believe that a major thunderstorm was on the way. I pulled off at an exit on the south side of Erie. I checked the RadarScope application on my phone. The line of storms was just to the west, and headed towards my location. I went inside a restaurant and bought something to eat as I waited for the storm to arrive. Then I began began video taping, filming to the west. As I filmed, the sky rapidly grew darker. A flag began standing straight out in the wind. Soon the winds were gusting so high that my car was shaking. Huge sheets of rain cascaded down, turning parts of the parking lot into flowing streams of water. Then, just a few minutes later, the rain stopped momentarily. I continued filming. Soon there was another heavy shower, of not just rain, but also small hail. "That's hail!" I exclaimed as I continued filming.

As the storm moved on to the east, I finished my dinner and prepared to head for home. I drove back home through moderate rain much of the way. Shortly after I crossed the border into New York, the rain ended, but it was overcast and cold, with temperatures in the 40's. I arrived back at my apartment just in time to take a brief walk before dark. Then I spent the rest of the evening viewing and editing my video of the storm and posting it on YouTube.

Contrary to my plans for a summer where I would work remotely and chase storms frequently, that was to be the my only storm chase for the year. I would be working remotely all right – but from home because I would not be allowed to drive for many weeks after my

HELLO, FREESWITCH!

Many of us have heard jokes about how geeks spend their Friday evenings. And I guess I am not much different. On the evening of my ruptured brain aneurysm, April 26, 2013, I had been busy setting up a software application known as FreeSWITCH. FreeSWITCH is a telephone PBX that works with VoIP (voice over internet). As a software developer, I like to stay current with technology and applications. And practically all of my life, I have been interested in phone systems. Years earlier, I set up a home PBX using another software product known as Asterisk. It was mostly a toy. I could call my PBX from a regular phone and listen in on sounds at my apartment. I could route calls to my home number to different destinations depending on the caller ID. So telemarketers would generally get obscure recordings that made them think there was a problem with the phone system, or find themselves in a series of never-ending menu options.

A friend of mine had recently mentioned that he used a different PBX known as FreeSWITCH. I thought I would go ahead and give it a try. As a challenge to help me get familiar with this new software, I decided to interface it with my old Asterisk system. The goal was to be able to dial into my Asterisk PBX from a landline phone, then be able to dial a particular extension and connect to the FreeSWITCH server. To avoid software conflicts between Asterisk and FreeSWITCH, I was installing FreeSWITCH on a different server I was renting in another state (i.e. a "cloud" server). Installation went smoothly, so I had turned my attention to interfacing between the two systems, the Asterisk system I had been running from my apartment for years and the FreeSWITCH system I had just set up on a server in Pennsylvania.

One issue I was having was that there were several phone systems involved, and as I dialed between them it was hard to tell where I had ended up. In North America, a standard dial tone is composed of two interfering tones, at 350 and 440 Hz. On my Asterisk system, I was using an old "City" dial tone, composed of the two frequencies 600 and 120 Hz (roughly the same frequencies as found in a modern busy signal). Since I was also using the "City" dial tone frequencies on the FreeSWITCH system I was setting up, I could not tell when dialing between the Asterisk system and the FreeSWITCH system whether the call had gone through to the dial tone of the FreeSWITCH system, or had somehow gotten bounced back to the Asterisk system. So I decided to modify the frequencies in the dial tone used by FreeSWITCH slightly. This would make the FreeSWITCH dial tone sound "off pitch" so it could be distinguished from the Asterisk dial tone. When I was connected to the telephone company system, I would hear a normal-sounding dial tone. When I was connected to my Asterisk system, I would hear and old "City" dial tone. And when I was connected to FreeSWITCH, I would hear a sick-sounding "off-key" dial tone. I heard that "off-key" dial tone many times that evening as I was setting up FreeSWITCH. It seems my brain came to associate that sick-sounding tone with what happened later that night (my ruptured brain aneurysm). The very sound of the off-key dial tone would make me feel physically ill and panicked after I got out of the hospital. In fact, I ended up dismantling the FreeSWITCH system soon after I got out of the hospital because it reminded me too strongly of the brain aneurysm. That would be perhaps the first sign of the post-traumatic stress issues I would later experience.

Once I had FreeSWITCH working and inter-operating with Asterisk, I took a shower, basking in the feeling of accomplishment. After the shower, I decided to give myself a haircut. Normally I would get a haircut on Saturday, but the next day (Saturday) I had plans to assist a local amateur radio club with spring cleanup. I was scheduled to fly to Virginia to visit my father and some friends just a few days later, and I wanted my hair cut before I left. So I got out my Norelco trimmer and began cutting my hair in front of the bathroom mirror. I put the stopper in the sink, and would bend down and let the hair fall into the sink. I'm wondering now if the pressure from bending down while cutting my hair may have been the final straw that caused my brain aneurysm to rupture.

Afterwards, I ran some more tests on FreeSWITCH. Since it was still too early for bed, I amused myself by watching various YouTube storm chasing videos. I became involved in the videos, and lost track of time. Soon I realized that it was getting late. I needed to be up early on Saturday to assist the ham club. Standing beside the bed, I set the alarm clock for 6:30AM. And that is the last thing I remember doing before my aneurysm ruptured.

The next thing I recall is apparently waking up from a deep sleep. I don't recall falling asleep, so I think I must have dozed off. Yet I am unable to open my eyes or move. I think maybe I'm dreaming. I keep trying to move, and I feel my legs move some. Gradually I am able to open my eyes. I find myself on the floor, beside the bed. The room appears dim and has somewhat of a red tinge to it. Am I dreaming? Awake? On some kind of drug? I don't know what to think. I realize I need to get help. Using all my strength, I am able to pull myself up onto the bed. I check my alarm clock. It has been about five minutes since I set the alarm. So I must have been unconscious for several minutes. As I lie on the bed, my strength starts returning. Soon I am able to get up. I walk to the kitchen. What the heck is going on? I pace back and forth in between the bedroom and kitchen. I try to remember what happened. I remember setting my alarm. Then I don't remember what happened after that. I realize I need to call help.

I call 911. The conversation goes something like this:

"911, what emergency situation do you wish to report, please?"

"Yes, uhm – I think I need to go to a hospital to be checked out. I was just getting ready for bed, and all of a sudden I found myself waking up, on the floor...."

"Do you think you had a heart attack?"

"I'm not sure – I'm not having any chest pain...."

"Ok, we will have an ambulance there shortly. Is the door unlocked?"

"No, it's locked, I'll answer the door."

"You might wish to go ahead and unlock it. That way they can get in if they need to."

"Okay, will do."

I realize I may be in the hospital for a while. So I get a few things together, including the charger for my phone. As it turns out, that phone was to become practically my only link to the rest of my world in the coming weeks.

In just a few minutes, there is a loud knock on the door. "Rescue!", I hear someone shout. I open the door. Rescue personnel ask me pretty much the same questions as the

911 dispatcher asked. Then they ask if I think I am strong enough to walk to the stretcher. "Of course!", I say. I get into the stretcher and am placed in the ambulance. They ask me where I want to go. Having not been in a hospital since early childhood, I have no idea which hospital is best. The rescue personnel recommend a place called the "MAC Center" (Mercy hospital Ambulatory Care). It is only a couple of miles away. There they can do tests and recommend an appropriate hospital.

As a police scanner listener, I am familiar with the transport procedure used by rescue personnel. What I hear the ambulance personnel say over their radio mike as the ambulance starts moving therefore sounds surreal to me. "We're en route to the MAC center with a 48-year old male patient, starting mileage is ....." I can't believe that this time, I am the patient! Very scary thought.

YOU'RE HAVING A STROKE

I was carried into the MAC center on a stretcher. Testing was quickly begun. First, I had wires taped to my chest for an EKG of my heart. The EKG showed no abnormalities. Then came a CAT scan of the head. I was placed on my back, and told to hold very still while my whole body was moved backwards so that my head was inside a round machine that would look at the inside of my brain. As I came out of the tube, I heard an alarm buzzer. The technician who was administering the scan yelled to someone "We've got a bleed!".

I tried to sit up to see what the technician was looking it. "Lay back down and be still!" he said. The technician looked very grim and somber. "Have you figured out what is wrong yet?", I asked. "Yes, it looks like you're having a stroke right now. I need you to lie back down and don't exert yourself anymore." I was told that I had a ruptured brain aneurysm, and would need to be taken to a hospital that specializes in treating strokes. An ambulance would be called to transport me to Mercy Hospital.

I knew this was serious. Back in the 1990's, I had worked with someone who had a ruptured brain aneurysm. He had missed several days of work at the end of one week due to severe headaches, and the following Monday we found out that he was in the hospital with a ruptured brain aneurysm. I remembered that they had to cut into his skull and do surgery on his brain, and that he was out of work for many weeks afterward. I recall passing his name on to the prayer chain at the church I attended at the time, after hearing that there was a significant chance that he could die. Yet I also recalled that he had eventually had made a complete recovery, and that six months later he was pretty much his "old self".

Upon arrival at Mercy Hospital, I needed to fill out many forms. The most disturbing of the forms asked questions about my desires regarding artificial life support, and next of kin to notify in case of my death. I was asked a bunch of questions about my medical history. A surgeon had been dispatched, I was told, and would be operating on me early in the morning. More forms to fill out regarding permission to perform various activities related to the surgery.

For close to twenty years, I had occasionally (every year or two) experienced symptoms of what doctors called a "silent migraine". These symptoms would always begin with a small blind spot near the center of my vision. Over the course of a few minutes, the blind spot would open up so I could see through it. The outer edges of it would have vibrating rainbow colors and appear irregular in shape. The shape would continue to open up as if I was looking through the center a squiggly, pulsating shape. Within a few more minutes, the shape would expand so much that its edges would move completely out of my field of vision. I had consulted two physicians, as well as an optometrist, about these scary symptoms. All three agreed that it was most likely simply a form of migraine. At the time of my ruptured aneurysm, it had been over a year (as I recall) since the last occurrence. Yet right after completing the forms, I noticed the blind spot developing in my vision. It evolved the same way as always, leaving behind a slight headache and mild nausea.

I was wheeled on a stretcher into a hospital room to wait for the surgeon to arrive. The TV was on in my room. I switched it to the weather channel. It was playing some unfamiliar song while weather reports scrolled by. I realized I had not watched anything on TV in many years.

Now it was close to 4AM. No one would be up yet, but I could send E-mails using my iPhone. I first sent an E-mail to my church asking to be added to the prayer list right away. Then I sent an E-mail to my boss at work, letting him know that I would likely be out of commission for quite some time. Finally I sent an E-mail to the radio club. I had promised to be there that morning to assist them with cleanup at the radio repeater site. That I would not be able to do.

My father normally calls me at around 7AM every Saturday morning. I knew he would be calling my home number, and would not get me. So at a few minutes before 7AM, I called him instead, using my cell phone. He was surprised to hear from me at the time he would normally call. "Where are you?", he said. "I'm at Mercy hospital...." "What happened to you?" I explained to him that I had a ruptured brain aneurysm. That the condition is serious, and that I "might even die, but I don't expect that". He wanted to confirm with me that I was "right with God". I told him I was.

Then he asked if I had ever gotten around to making I will. That I had not. And I was nervous about that. I have no brothers or sisters, and the relatives I am close to are all elderly. In 25 years of working, I had accumulated a fairly sizable number of investments. I planned to divide these among various charities. Images of most of the money ending up in the hands of lawyers, with what little remained being split up among distant relatives I didn't even know, filled my head. My father recommended that I "call a lawyer" and have him come to the hospital to make out a will. But I knew I would not be up to doing that, since I had not thought much about the specifics and had no idea who I would want to execute my will.

So while I was not concerned about my eternal spiritual fate, I was quite concerned about how earthly matters would play out in the case of my death.

LOTS OF BEAUTIFUL SUNRISES

Just minutes after I got off the phone with my father, the surgeon arrived for my emergency surgery. I was placed on a stretcher and rushed downstairs on the elevator to the surgery room. That room looked to me like an industrial shop of some kind. It was filled with machines. The ceiling was not a real ceiling, but one like you would find in a warehouse. There was a long tubular device – big enough to contain an entire body – that looked similar to a CAT scan machine. Beside it were several large TV screens full of medical images. There were more forms to sign to consent to each of the surgical procedures the surgeon would be using.

The first step of surgery for a ruptured brain aneurysm is to look at the aneurysm in detail. To do this, a catheter is is first inserted in a large leg artery near the groin (femoral artery). This catheter is then navigated through the artery up to the area of the brain where the aneurysm is located. A special contrast dye is released from the catheter to allow for imaging of the aneurysm. Once a clear picture of the aneurysm is available, the surgeon is able to decide on an appropriate treatment. If the aneurysm has a wide neck or irregular shape, then cranial surgery (opening up the skull and placing a clip around the aneurysm to stop the bleeding) is required. Back in the 1990s, cranial surgery was pretty much the only option. But in recent years, a procedure known as "coiling" has become possible for many aneurysms. During the coiling procedure, platinum coils of wire are navigated through the catheter and placed in the aneurysm. These coils cause the blood to clot in the aneurysm, thus stopping the bleeding. The coiling procedure is usually done using only local anesthesia. Thus the patient is fully awake throughout the surgery (although sedatives may be given to decrease anxiety).

In my case, the right femoral artery was used. The surgeon navigated the catheter up to the aneurysm and was able to determine that coiling was a viable option. I was so nervous while the procedure was going on that my arms and legs were shaking uncontrollably despite some sedation being given. "HOLD STILL!!!" the surgeon kept shouting. I kept mumbling "I'm trying, I'm trying!". I heard the doctor curse upon seeing the latest image. It showed that the coiling device had missed the aneurysm due to my motion. He would have to try again. On the second try, he was able to reach the aneurysm and insert coils successfully.

I was told that the surgery had been successful. Even so, the risks were just beginning. When a brain aneurysm ruptures, blood flows into the the area between the brain and skull (known as the subarachnoid space). This blood can damage nearby parts of the brain directly in the days following the hemorrhage. It can also cause nearby blood vessels to constrict, resulting in a stroke. There is also the possibility that blood is able to leak past the coils, resulting in another bleeding. I was hooked up to two IVs, one in each arm. A catheter was also inserted into my penis so I would not have to get out of bed to urinate. Electrodes were placed on my chest to allow continuous heart monitoring, and to allow for quick defibrillator access should heart problems occur due to the shock from the brain bleed.

Instead of being taken back to my original hospital room, I was now taken to the Intensive Care Unit. Intensive Care is located on the very top floor of the hospital, away from other patients, to allow for much closer monitoring than for normal hospital patients. My room faced east. As I was being wheeled into the room, the technician said to me "Well, one good thing about this is that you are on the top floor. You have an excellent view. You are going to be seeing lots of beautiful sunrises."

Using my cell phone, I called my father to let him know that the initial surgery had been successful. After that, the only thing I wanted to do was rest. Besides exhaustion and shock from the aneurysm and surgery itself, I had not slept at all the previous night. I knew vaguely that the danger was just starting, but figured it would do no good to worry about it. The thing I needed to do most to help with my recovery was sleep.

The next few days passed quickly as I slept most of the time, and are mostly a blur in my memory. But I remember a few things. Each morning at around 5AM, a nurse would wake me up to do a cranial Doppler scan. This procedure, which took about a half hour or so, involved placing transducers on various points of by neck and head and taking measurements. These measurements allow the blood flow through various blood vessels in the brain to be determined. The readings are important, because blood vessels tend to constrict in nearby brain areas following a brain bleed. This can result in a secondary stroke. An hour or two later, usually between 6AM and 7AM, my surgeon would come in to check on me. Not only would he check my vitals and the results of the Doppler scans, he would also examine how the femoral artery on my leg was healing, and discuss how I was doing with me. After seeing the surgeon, I would generally check E-mails using my phone. Some days I would talk to others (such as my father) by phone. I would check the weather forecast and sometimes watch the news on TV. Then breakfast would come. After eating, I would sleep again until someone woke me up to tell me it was time for lunch. I would eat lunch and then sleep again until time for dinner. After dinner, I would check my E-mails again, browse web sites online, and watch TV until bedtime.

Each day, the nurse would write the date on a white board at the front of my hospital room. I was amazed at how quickly time was passing. My brain aneurysm rupture occurred on April 26th. Soon I was looking at the word "May" in dates on the white board. I didn't know how long I would need to stay. I notified my cat sitter that I was still in the hospital and needed her to continue to visit daily to feed and play with my cat Patrick. I kept in touch with my boss and friends via E-mail.

Nurses and technicians would come in frequently to ask me questions that are typically asked of stroke patients. "How are you feeling?" "What day is this?" "Can you tell me where you are?" "How many fingers am I holding up?" "Can you count backward from 100 for me?" "Who is the current president?" "Squeeze my fingers as hard as you can with your right hand. Now with your left hand." "I'm going to push on your foot. Try to keep me from pushing it in". In each case, I had no trouble with the questions and tasks, and found them a bit silly. But I realize that aneurysm and stroke patients can suffer delayed effects from bleeding in the brain, so it made sense that they frequently ask questions such as these.

One question I was asked after several days was when was the last time I had had a bowel movement. I had not had one since I was admitted to the hospital. I was told that this was somewhat normal because I was inactive and confined to bed, but that I would be given a laxative to solve the problem. Sure enough, a few hours later, I needed to have a bowel movement. I rang for the nurse. "Where is the restroom around here?", I asked. "You're in intensive care; there is no rest room.", she said. "Well, soon I need to have a bowel movement! What am I supposed to do?", I said. "We have a portable toilet we can bring in if necessary."

While my surgeon was happy with the recovery process from my brain aneurysm coiling, he was not happy with how the femoral artery on my right leg (where the surgery had been done from) was healing. Apparently, following the surgery, blood had continued to flow beneath the skin. The upper part of my right leg was now completely black and blue – it looked like my leg had been run over by something. The doctor explained that I had developed "an aneurysm" in my, uhm, "groin area" as a result of the surgery. It was continuing to bleed. Joking, he said, "Everyone needs at least two aneurysms you know – one in the brain, and the other in the groin!" "Yeah", I said, "And I'm sure I think with both of mine!" After some further looking at the aneurysm in my leg, I was scheduled for minor surgery that evening to stop the remaining blood flow. That surgery was done right in my hospital room, and was uneventful.

After a few more days of doing nothing but lying in bed, my surgeon said he wanted me to start getting out of bed and sitting in a chair while I ate lunch. I thought I would be glad to do this, but as it turned out, my neck was extremely sore from the surgery. Sitting in a chair caused intense pain in my neck, and I could not wait to get back in bed so I could rest my neck. My surgeon said this was a normal result of my surgery, but that I still needed to try to sit up as long as possible to help with my healing. The first day I was only able to accomplish a few minutes of sitting up in the chair before I could not stand the pain any longer and needed to go back to bed. On the second day, I wanted to try longer. My personal goal was to sit in the chair for 20 minutes. As I concentrated on eating my lunch, the pain was bearable. But once I was done eating, my thoughts turned back to my pain, and I didn't think I would be able to sit for the remaining time. But right as I was going to call the nurse for help getting back in bed, I was told I had a visitor. A visitor! Who could it be? I was excited. Two fellows from work were escorted into my room. I felt a bit embarrassed. Here I was, sitting in a chair with just hospital pajamas on, and the long tube from a catheter running to a large urine collection basin beside my bed. But I was happy to see my friends, and soon forgot my self-consciousness. "I just had to stop by and see you.", one of them said. "I kept calling the hospital and they said only close relatives were allowed to visit. I kept calling back to ask when you would be able to have other visitors, and they were giving me the run-around, so I decided I would come down here and see for myself. When I got here, I told them that you don't have any close relatives nearby, and that we are close friends from work, so they let me in." They wanted to know exactly what had happened, so I described how I experienced my brain aneurysm on April 26th. I asked them how things were going at work. Before I knew it, nearly an hour had passed. They were on lunch break at work, so they headed back. And I had sat up for over an hour without experiencing the neck pain! I called the nurse for assistance getting back in bed, overflowing with a sense of accomplishment at having sat up for so

very blessed to have so many people writing such caring remarks about me. I placed the poster in a prominent place in front of the room, where I would see it every time I sat up in bed.

OUT OF ICU

Each morning, my surgeon would visit with me to monitor my progress. One of my nurses started to act as sort of an advocate for me. She said I would need to actively request permission to take small steps to return back towards normality. One morning, she asked, "Can the urine catheter be removed?" No response from the surgeon. The same thing happened the second day. On the third day, the surgeon gave his approval for the urine catheter to be removed. So it was removed that afternoon. This was a mixed blessing. Although I was not drinking an excessive amount of fluids, I was on two IVs that put quite a lot of fluid into me. In fact, part of the treatment following a ruptured brain aneurysm involves increasing blood volume and blood pressure. This helps prevent a secondary stroke from occurring due to reduced blood flow through the brain that can be caused by left over blood from the hemorrhage. As a result, I found myself needing to urinate every couple hours. I quickly filled two large containers that were kept by my bed for this purpose, and frequently had to call to have them emptied. Despite this inconvenience and its effect on sleep, I was happy that I was making slow but steady progress. Not having the catheter also meant one less connection to worry about if I wished to get up from bed.

I asked the doctor when I would be able to leave the Intensive Care Unit and go to a normal room. He said that presently, my blood pressure and blood volume were being raised for preventative purposes, and that doing this required careful monitoring that was only available in the ICU. However, he said he thought that this procedure should only be required for a few more days, and that after that I should be able to move to a normal hospital room. Using my iPhone, I frequently communicated with friends and co-workers via E-mail. I sent out a message that said something like "Good news – Doctor says I can likely move from ICU to regular room in a few days". When the move was delayed in coming days, I wrote E-mails about how dismayed I was. I wanted more than anything to get back to normal as soon as possible, and getting out of ICU would be a big step in that direction. Finally one morning, after nearly 2 weeks in the ICU, my surgeon let me know that I would be transferred to a regular room later that day.

I proudly gathered up my belongings for the move to a different room. I placed the Get Well poster the kids had made for me in a prominent location at the front of my new room.

The regular hospital room had a toilet. I was shown how to unplug my IV machine (it had a battery backup that allowed it to continue operating even when unplugged) so I could take it with me when I needed to get up to go to the restroom. Walking to the restroom, or anyplace else for that matter, was far more difficult than I had expected. I've always enjoyed walking. At the time my brain aneurysm ruptured, I was walking at least six miles every day. Yet after two weeks of being in bed all the time, my legs had become very weak. Just standing up took me over a minute, and walking itself was at a snail's pace. Besides the weakness in both legs, my right leg was severely bruised where the blood had continued to flow under the skin after my operation. It literally looked like that leg has been run over by a truck, and the bruising had even spread to my groin area and the lower part of my stomach. Proudly though of my my new ability to take care of personal needs myself, I shuffled my way to the bathroom under the watchful eye of the nurse. As I stood up to use the bathroom, she commented, "You might want to sit down. It's safer."

Another feature of a regular hospital room was that I would have a roommate. But initially, there was no one else in my room. I looked forward to having a roommate to talk to, especially now that I was receiving less attention from the staff due to being out of the ICU. A real disadvantage of being single and not having any relatives nearby was not having anyone to talk to. While I did get a few visits from work friends and church staff, most days I spent by myself, with only E-mail, the web, and the TV to keep my company the majority of the time.

Around the middle of the morning on Friday May 10th, I got my first roommate. He was a professional-looking guy, who appeared to be in his early 40's. Once he got settled in the room, I quickly began asking him about himself. The room I was in was in the stroke care area of the hospital. I found it hard to believe that someone that young could be recovering from a stroke. "What brings you here?", I asked. "Well, my body just decided that I was going to spend the weekend in a hospital. Guess I'll be here at least through Sunday.", he said. He then went on to describe the events of that morning. He had been shaving, and he noticed one side of his body felt like it was reacting slower than normal. He had then driven to work, and noticed that he had trouble steering the car with his left arm. When he got to work, his boss noticed his difficulties and insisted he go to the hospital to be checked out. His boss had driven him. His wife and son, he said, had been notified, and would be visiting him later in the day. I briefly described the ordeal I had just experienced with the ruptured brain aneurysm, and how just the day before I had finally been able to transfer from the ICU to a normal hospital room. After a bit of further discussion, my new acquaintance turned his attention to contacting relatives and friends using his cell phone. I heard him repeat the story of what had happened to him that day over and over to each of them. I felt somehow connected with him, since he also had had a stroke, and I was curious as to how things would go for him given that he had a wife, family, and relatives in town.

Late that afternoon, as I watched weather radar using an app on my phone, a few minor thunderstorms developed in the area. And I was excited. At home, my newest lightning detector was online, monitoring for strikes. This would be a chance to test it. I tried to remember if there was some way I could connect remotely to my the computer at home that the detector was connected to. I had not set up any specific way to do this, because I never expected to be away from home for so long. But I seemed to recall that I had set up a remote connection to that computer previously for some other experiment. I just needed to remember the details of how to connect, and what the password was. I kept racking my brain to figure out how. And I kept jumping up to look out the window when I thought I saw lightning. I was getting exhausted from all the physical and mental effort. But it was what I wanted to do. It felt good to concentrate on something besides my health for once.

As the rain and lightning were ending and evening beginning, my new acquaintance's wife, son, and assorted other relatives, arrived to visit him. His son was about 12 years old. He didn't seem real concerned, acting pretty much like a normal 12-year-old in front of his dad. His biggest concern seemed to be getting a snack from the hospital concession stand. His wife and other relatives were more concerned though. Though minor, the stroke had been in a critical area of the brain known as the pons area. This area, located in the brainstem, controls such major body areas as the heart and breathing, so even a minor stroke in this area is considered serious. Him and his wife were discussing the prognosis. He would have to make some lifestyle changes. Less stress, less drinking.

Lifestyle factors can influence the chances for having a stroke. Such factors as poor diet, smoking, excessive alcohol consumption, and high stress can increase the probability of having a stroke. In my case, it the biggest risk was likely due to being born with the congenital condition Bicuspid Aortic Valve. That condition increases the changes of having a brain aneurysm by over ten times. Of course, stress may well have been a factor in my ruptured brain aneurysm, but my diet and exercise were good. Not true for most stroke victims, especially when stroke occurs at an early age.

As the hours passed, the conversation between my new acquaintance and his guests grew less serious and more lively. After his son had left, some off-color jokes were even exchanged. Suddenly, one of the ladies in the group looked uneasily over at me. By this time, I was paying little attention. But I heard one of them whisper "Shh, watch your language! I think that guy is a priest!" I looked at her. "Are you a priest?", she asked me in a subdued voice. "No, I'm a software developer – what made you think I am a priest?" She said she saw the Get Well poster that the kids had made for me. I explained that I was also a teacher, and that my kids had made the poster. Shyly, the guest asked if I had been offended by the language. I told her not to worry about it, and that I heard far more course jokes than that at work.

Though I now had a roommate, I still had my own TV. I settled into my usual routine of watching it. This was new to me – I had not watched television (except for YouTube) more than a few hours total over the past year. First I watched the Weather Channel. Once the weather channel switched from weather reporting to drama shows, I switched to financial news and finally to news. My roommate watched a sitcom on his TV. At 10PM, I turned my TV off and prepared to go to sleep. Shortly after that, my roommate turned off his TV as well. He connected what he said was a "sleeping machine", explaining that he has sleep apnea and that he has to use the machine or else he has breathing issues while sleeping.

Although I was no longer in Intensive Care, my nurse still woke me up every few hours to take my scheduled medicine doses. "Is my horse pill ready?", I asked, referring to one particularly large pill that I took two of every four hours. Shortly after taking the 2AM dose of my medicines, something aroused me again. It was a nurse trying to wake my roommate up. It turned out that my roommate has a naturally low pulse rate. When he sleeps, it drops even lower. This had triggered an alarm. Upon waking, my roommate explained his history of a low pulse rate to the nurse. She did a few measurements, then seemed satisfied and left.

HAPPY MOTHER'S DAY!

I was developing increasing confidence the first couple days that I was in a regular room. I could use the restroom by myself. And I was working at strengthening my legs. It no longer took me a minute or two to stand up. My surgeon had advised that I not just practice standing, but practice sitting down and getting up. So that's what I was doing. As I watched the room TV in the evenings, I would stand up, then sit down, then stand back up. I was doing this dozens of times each day, and it was helping. I could now stand up within a few seconds, instead of the minute or two it took me the first few times I tried standing in the ICU. Once a day, a physical therapist would stop by to take me on longer walks, using a cane. We would walk the length of the hospital floor. One time she even had me go up a flight of stairs.

Yet there was one thing that was not quite right. Sometimes as I walked, I started feeling a bit light-headed. It only lasted a few seconds, and as I continued on it would go away on its own. I mentioned this in passing to the physical therapist. She said it was probably that I was not used to being upright for so long, after having laid in a hospital bed continuously for close to two weeks. I also felt a bit foggy mentally at times. But that was attributed to a high dose of an anti-seizure medicine (levetiracetam) I was on. When the brain is disturbed by bleeding and subsequent surgery, it is standard preventative procedure for the patient to be placed on anti-seizure medication for a month or more, followed by a slow taper. Side effects of this medicine can include a decrease in coordination, as well as tiredness and slowed mental functioning. It acts in a similar way to a tranquilizer. So I assumed the light-headed symptoms were being caused by either not being used to being in an upright position for so long, or to the levetiracetam, or a combination of both. All physical and mental functioning tests were evaluating my condition as excellent. I had no problems with moving any part of my body, and no problems thinking or remembering things. I was very thankful.

One evening, when I was feeling particularly confident, I asked my surgeon if he thought I might be able to go home soon. I was excited when he said I might be able to leave in just a few more days. He asked me if I was happy with how I was improving, and I said yes. When he asked me specifically why I thought I was better now, there was no question in my mind. I was much more mobile, and I could stand up in a small fraction of the time it had taken just a week earlier.

Sunday May 12 was Mother's day. Starting in the early morning, the hospital was filled with numerous visitors.

My roommate's wife stopped by along with a bunch of relatives. I was scheduled to talk to my father by phone for the first time in several days. Since this call fell on a Sunday, he had requested that we talk later in the morning instead of at the usual 6:30 or 7:00AM so that he would have time to get ready for and attend church. With all the Mother's Day activity going on around me, I felt a bit lonely.

Right after breakfast, I requested from the nurse a new hospital gown. I had worn the same gown for several days, and it now had some food stains. Since there were so many visitors coming and going for Mother's Day, I thought it might be best if I changed my gown in the bathroom. I did leave the bathroom door open, though. As I finished taking off the old gown, I saw my roommate approach the bathroom. He was carrying a shaver, and apparently was waiting for me to finish in the bathroom so he could go in there and start shaving. This was the first time I had changed my hospital gown without assistance, and I was a bit confused. It turns out there were two identical gowns. One is to be worn forward, and the other backwards. Both gowns have to then be tied. And I couldn't figure it out. I kept taking them back off and starting over. I could see my roommate waiting patiently at the door, and I was getting nervous that I was holding him up. As I struggled with the gowns, I began to feel light-headed. But I decided to persevere.

The next thing I remember is a nurse shaking me and asking if I was okay. At first, I thought I was waking up from a night's sleep, but then I realized I was laying of the floor and realized that the last thing I remembered was struggling with my hospital gown.

My surgeon poked his head in the room almost immediately. The nurse said something to the effect that my blood pressure has been extremely low, but was starting to go up now. My surgeon immediately ordered an IV administered "at the fastest rate possible on the machine". I was returned to bed and told not to get out of bed anymore without someone watching me. I was also told that an emergency scan of my brain was being arranged, and I would be taken down on a cart when it was available.

Soon after I was put back into bed, my cell phone started ringing. The caller ID showed it was my father. I let it go to voice mail. I was too dazed by what had just happened to have my wits about me and talk on the phone. I felt concerned and demoralized by the new problem as well. I would wait until after the emergency scan when I had more information before talking to him. As I laid there a few minutes later, the cell phone rang again. It was someone from the hospital staff. My father was on the phone with the hospital staff and wanted to know the correct number to call me at. I explained to the lady taking the call that I was feeling too disoriented to talk on the phone at the time.

Upon hearing this from the receptionist, my father talked to other hospital staff to check on how I was doing. He asked for information about me, and was told that "he fell". When he asked if it was a serious fall, they said "We don't know. We just know he fell."

I gradually calmed down over the course of the next couple hours. My roommate was alone now. All his guests had left. He told me that he had called the nurse when he saw me fall. "I knew something was wrong even before that.", he said. "You were moving around very slowly and fumbling with the hospital gown like you were really confused. I was going to yell for a nurse and then you fell with a loud 'thud'". I thanked my roommate for being prepared and calling help right away.

A short while later, a nurse came in and said it was time for my scan. I was wheeled into an elevator down to the floor where the scan equipment was located. The scan was completed in a few minutes, and I was brought back to my hospital bed. "Remember, do NOT get out of bed without someone there to watch you", she reminded me. I was told that a doctor would be interpreting the results of the scan, and that my surgeon would see me to explain the results when they were ready. By this point, I was feeling close to normal mentally. I began trying to figure out what might have happened. I tried not to worry about it being something serious.

Soon my surgeon came in to tell me his findings. It turns out I was suffering from "hydrocephalus" - excessive accumulation of fluid on the brain. The brain and spinal cord are surrounded by a clear liquid called cerebrospinal fluid. This fluid serves to protect the brain from shock.

After any type of stroke, excess amounts of this fluid can be produced, or the normal flow of the fluid can be blocked. The excess fluid pressure can result in lightheadedness. He explained that this condition might be temporary as a result of my ruptured brain aneurysm and surgery. If that was the case, a single draining of the excess fluid should resolve the problem. If, however, it did not, I would need to have a permanent shunt installed in my head to drain the excess fluid. This, of course, would be another major surgical procedure.

I called my father to let him know the findings. I had not E-mailed any of my friends about my latest complication, so decided not to mention anything to them for now. Shortly after dinner, a doctor arrived for the operation. This was considered minor surgery, and could be performed right in my hospital room. By this time, my roommate had several guests in the room again. The doctor explained that a surgical procedure was going to be performed in the hospital room, and therefore that the guests needed to leave for now. I was given more paperwork to authorize the surgery.

The surgery involved sticking a needle into my spinal cord area, and draining a measured amount of fluid. It was done under local anesthesia. Though the thought of what was actually occurring in the procedure was disconcerting, the procedure was not particularly painful. Within about a half hour, the procedure was complete. I felt exhausted afterwards, after an emotionally long day, but physically I was now feeling okay.

Observation over the coming days, as well as additional brain scans, indicated that the operation had been successful. The fluid was no longer building up excessive pressure in my brain, so no further treatment would be required. And I was very thankful for that.

HOMEWARD BOUND

After the Mother's Day scare, I continued improving. There were no more issues with hydrocephalus. My neurologist began to talk about scheduling my release. There was concern about my ability to handle being at home alone, due to my right leg injury. I was able to walk with a cane, but since I have a third floor apartment, it was uncertain if I would be able to negotiate the four flights of stairs. With the physical therapist at the hospital, I practiced climbing stairs. I personally was confident of my physical ability, but the hospital wanted to be sure before releasing me.

Besides physical challenges, brain aneurysm survivors often suffer mental deficits that can interfere with daily activities. So it is normal to test not only the patient's physical abilities, but also their mental abilities prior to release. I was still taking the anti-seizure medicine levetiracetam. This medicine acts in similar ways to a tranquilizer, and can slow down thinking. Nonetheless, I was confident of my mental abilities. I remember as part of one of the tests I was asked what I would do if there was a fire in my kitchen. As the geek I am, I had actually experienced a small fire in my kitchen once while doing an experiment. The temptation was for me to recall that incident and reply something like "I would turn off the power supply and let the molten chemicals cool." I was feeling pretty cocky now that I was feeling better and would be going home soon. But of course I knew that would in fact raise questions about my mental state. So I gave the standard answer. I would turn off the stove, and if necessary use the fire extinguisher that I keep in my kitchen to put out the fire.

Before I could be released from the hospital, my blood chemistry would need to be checked. With all the different medicines and IVs given at the hospital, blood chemistry is often disrupted. This would need to be corrected prior to release. The blood tests revealed that I had a very low potassium level. So they had me add large potassium supplement pills to the medicines I took every 4 hours. A day or so later, they did another blood test and measured the potassium levels again. And it was still very low. So I would need to be given extra potassium by IV. Unfortunately, because potassium is critical to heart function, getting a potassium IV means that one has to have their heart monitored continuously as a precaution. So I would again be connected to more wires, for the first time since my early days in the ICU.

Potassium IVs are actually somewhat painful, and they often cause bruising at the IV Site. I developed a noticeable bruise on my arm after 24 hours of continuous potassium IVs. The extra fluid from the IVs also resulted in frequent urination, which was a problem particularly at night. It was then time for another blood test. The test showed that my potassium was still too low. This meant more IVs, and more time connected to the heart monitor. The doctors were pretty sure, however, that these should be the last IVs I would need. It was to be one more night of discomfort. But the next morning, the IVs were complete.

Some of the contacts from my heart monitor were falling off that morning. I figured with the IVs complete, I didn't need the monitor anymore. So I removed the remainder of the contacts and took off the device. A few minutes later, a nurse came in. "Your heart monitor seems to have stopped working.", she said. "Yes, several of the contacts fell off, so I took it off. The IVs are done now anyway." She immediately put it back on me. "Your potassium is low! You need to have your heart monitored at all times!", she exclaimed. "And, you shouldn't be getting up and walking without someone watching you, since your heart is being monitored!", she said. I felt discouraged. The date was May 16th, the date I had originally been tentatively scheduled for release. I knew a nurse had drawn blood earlier in the morning. Was my potassium level still too low? And now I wasn't even supposed to get up to use the restroom by myself? Things were not looking good.

Less than an hour later, the nurse came back in and told me I could remove the heart monitor. "Your test results are back, and the doctor says everything looks good." My neurologist came in to see me a short while later. He told me I would be released from the hospital later in the day.

Who would come and get me from the hospital? I have no relatives who live nearby. One of my co-workers might be able to do it, but I didn't know what time I would be released, and didn't feel comfortable having them miss potentially a lot of work time waiting for me. Besides, the hospital, and my apartment, were not particularly convenient to the office where I worked. So a few days before I was to be released, I let the pastor at my church know that I was looking for someone who would be willing to take me home from the hospital when the time came. Two ladies who I had taught Sunday School with previously volunteered. I contacted one of them. Unfortunately, I didn't know what time I would be released. So I couldn't give a definite time. But I told her I would give her as much advance notice as possible, and work with her schedule.

There was one other complication. Shortly after lunch, I developed a moderate headache. While headaches are extremely common after a ruptured brain aneurysm, I had not had any headaches prior to this. Although not particularly painful, I was concerned what the headache might mean. It seemed like this was the worst possible time for me to develop a headache, because I would no longer be at the hospital being monitored if something was in fact wrong. My surgeon ordered another brain scan. While awaiting the results of the scan late that afternoon, my headache continued. A nurse asked me if I had taken any pain medication. Although since early on they had given me pain pills to take "as needed", I had not taken any up to this point. I wanted to take as few different medicines as possible, especially something potentially addictive such as pain killers. However, the nurse said that it was my surgeon's recommendation that I go ahead and take pain medicine for the headache. Great, I thought. Now I'm going to be on "hard drugs", and if I do get released later I will be drugged up. But I did go ahead and take the pain medicine. Within a half hour, the headache was gone, although I did feel somewhat groggy.

The brain scan came back good. After dinner, I was told that I would be released within a couple hours, as soon as the doctors completed the necessary paperwork. I contacted my ride home. Hospital security came to my room to return my wallet and other belongings. I had signed a list of the belongings that had taken for safekeeping upon my admission to the hospital. They went over the list, and counted out the money in my wallet. An hour or so later, I was told to get my clothes on and call my ride. I struggled to get my clothes on, particularly my pants and shoes. Not only was my right leg badly bruised and painful, but my feet were swollen from both lack of use and from all the fluid in the IVs.

Veronica arrived to pick me up. A nurse went over my discharge instructions, which included numerous prescription medicines I would need to take every four hours. I signed my release papers. With my cane in my hand, I was wheeled to the parking lot where Veronica helped me get into her van.

The ride home was surreal. It had been three weeks since I had seen the outside world. Plus, I was experiencing mental effects from the levetiracetam, as well as the pain pills I had taken a few hours earlier. The outside world was whizzing by, and it all seemed like a dream. But I needed to keep my wits about me. We needed to to stop by a pharmacy to pick up a whole list of prescription medicines before they closed. And I would then be facing the most difficult physical task of getting up four flights of stairs. As we approached the pharmacy, we saw someone Veronica knew from church. "Guess who I have with me?", she said. I waved.

Walking from the car to the pharmacy was slow and awkward with my cane. I handed the pharmacist my stash of prescription orders to be filled, and slowly walked around the store with Veronica while waiting for them to be ready. Then the walk back out to the car was again slow and awkward. I realized just how disabled I was. Lying in bed or sitting in a chair in the hospital while E-mailing people on my cell phone or watching TV, I had felt like I was pretty close to normal. Now seeing my physical challenges and mental slowness due to the medicines made me lose confidence somewhat in my abilities.

We arrived at my apartment. I felt like I was under pressure now. I needed to get up the stairs, and I didn't want to take any more of Veronica's time than necessary. Then I would face going into my own house, and figuring out how to be self-sufficient for the first time in weeks. Plus I would need to figure out the schedules for all the medicines I needed to take, and arrange to wake up every four hours to take them. But at the same time, I was very excited that I would get to see my cat for the first time in three weeks. I made my way up the stairs without too much difficulty, holding on to the rails. I found my key, opened the door, and was immediately greeted by cat Patrick. Veronica stayed a few minutes, then said goodbye, and told me to call her if I needed anything.

So I was finally home! I decided it would be best to leave my door unlocked. There is a common entrance to my apartment, and then doors to each individual apartment. If I experienced problems and had to call rescue, I wanted to make sure they could get in. No one who I did not know had ever tried to open my door before, so I felt it was safest to leave it unlocked. I hung my name band from the hospital on the door knob. I figured that way, rescuers would be able to get information about my recent hospitalization quickly if needed.

The first thing I did was make sense of all my medicine schedules. I created a list of what I needed to take at each particular time, and I arranged for an alarm to go off every four hours so I could wake up and take the medicines I needed to take. I wrote a brief (few sentence) entry in my diary. I had not written anything in 20 days – by far the longest time since I began keeping a diary years ago as a child. I felt incredibly content, lying in my bed with my cat beside me. I stayed up just thinking and enjoying his presence.

Around 1AM, I turned off the light. Normally I close my bedroom door so my cat does not disturb my sleep. But after having been alone for the past 3 weeks, I felt my cat deserved to spend the night with me that night. That was somewhat of a mistake. Several times during the night, Patrick jumped up onto the bed, landing on my sore leg and waking me up. And I needed to get up to take medicines every 4 hours. Still, I was getting better sleep than in the hospital. I was incredibly thankful to be home at last.

WALK WITH A CANE

For the first few days after I was released from the hospital, I needed to take some of medicines every 4 hours. That meant setting an alarm to wake up in the middle of the night. I was very tired in the initial days home from the hospital. Not only was my body requiring extra resources for healing, particularly my leg, but also because it is hard to sleep in a hospital. Many people imagine that a hospital stay might be a good way to catch up on sleep. But that is not the case. A hospital is a busy place, particularly in the ICU. Emergencies happen, and nurses and doctors can be heard rushing around. Once in a regular room, roommates need to get up or be administered medicine. Medical tests, such as the transcranial Doppler scans I had done daily, happen around 5AM. My first night home from the hospital was probably my best nights sleep since my brain aneurysm ruptured three weeks earlier. In fact, it was probably the best I had slept in months – or maybe even years. The first few nights home from the hospital, I would go to bed as early as 9PM, and sleep in as late at 9AM. That was completely unheard of for me. My normal sleep schedule prior to my hospitalization was to go to bed between 11:30 and get up around 6:30. I am actually a morning person, and would prefer to go to bed and get up at least an hour earlier than that, but dealing with multiple time zones on the job meant I had to shift my day to later hours like the above. Once I was no longer waking up every four hours to take medicines, I began getting up near normal time, but was still going to bed at the earlier hour.

On my first full day home from the hospital, my biggest desire was to take a good, long bath. And to shave. I had not been able to take a bath or shower while in the hospital. I was able to wash up with a cloth, but that does not do a good job. Razors are generally kept out of the hospital for fear of bleeding problems with patients taking blood thinners. I knew I looked and smelled horrible. I spent a couple of hours in the tub that day. I filled the tub several times, and each time I would wash a little more. Getting in and out of the tub was a bit difficult with my right leg being so badly bruised, and my left leg still weak from lack of use. I knew I had to be careful not to slip – something that had never really concerned me before. I spent many minutes shaving as well. It felt good to feel clean and groomed for the first time in weeks.

Now looking presentable, that afternoon I decided to venture out of my apartment for the first time. There is a road loop that goes around my apartment complex. It is several blocks long. My goal was to walk around the entire length of that loop. I knew it would take me a long time to get all the way around, but then that would be my physical exercise for the day. Cane in hand, I slowly made my way down the steps and to the door. Walking at a fraction of a mile per hour, I made it out the door to the road loop. I slowly began to make my way down the road. I had my doubts. "I'm really pushing myself too hard", I thought. What if I get halfway around the loop and then don't have the strength to get the rest of the way back? About 15 minutes and a block down, I considered turning back. I was already getting a bit tired. "No sense in pushing it", I thought. But I kept going, and it actually felt like the walking got easier after that. On my way around the loop, I saw an old man walking with a cane. It gave me a very strange and distressing feeling. I was now like this old man!

Since I was not allowed to drive yet, someone from church offered to take me to the grocery store one evening. My first trip to the grocery store was slow and exhausting. Using my grocery cart as a walker did help a bit, but it took me close to an hour to get all the groceries I needed. I knew I should stock up on things since I would not be allowed to drive for a while. My appetite was good in my early days home from the hospital, and I was thankful to be eating my own choice of food again.

Over the following few days, my walking ability improved markedly. I no longer needed the cane, although I still needed to hold tightly onto the rails when going up or down steps. After about a week of walking practice, going a few blocks up the road and back, I was ready to do my first walking to accomplish a specific task by myself. I would walk to Subway, which is around a half mile away, get lunch, and then walk back. Again, I was nervous. I had to cross a major street to get there, but at least there was a stop light for pedestrians. People at Subway might notice my slow walking, and the limp in my right leg. Then they might ask what happened, and I would have to tell them all about the brain aneurysm. I didn't want to do that; the brain aneurysm was something I wanted to forget and put behind me. Though slowly, and with considerable nervousness, I did mange to walk to Subway, order lunch, eat it there, and walk back. I felt good that I had actually accomplished that task, and was slowly becoming independent again. The next day was Sunday, and I was able to walk to and attend my church (which is about 1 mile away).

I returned to work, full time, less than a week after I got out of the hospital. I was not allowed to drive, but I am able to work from home when needed. I wanted to get back to work partly to keep my mind off what had happened. I had previously read books that say those suffering a loss or traumatic event recover faster when they have family to care for. I don't have family, but I felt that getting back to work would be doing something for someone else and thus help keep my mind off myself. Besides that, I was getting lonely not interacting with others. And finally, I had missed three weeks of work. I didn't have any more sick time left. And I knew there was a ton of stuff that needed to be done at work. In retrospect, going back to work full-time so soon was the wrong decision. I still had frequent doctor appointments to arrange and go to, plus dealing with insurance claims and issues. Plus I was still sleeping more than normal. But the trauma had caused me to lose interest in my hobbies, and work was a good way to spend my time, so I thought.

At a doctor's appointment a couple weeks later, my surgeon was extremely surprised that I was already working full-time. When I visited my primary care doctor for a debriefing on the aneurysm and told him I was working from home, his first comment was "Is anyone checking to see if your work is actually correct?". Well, I think the work was mostly correct. In software development, one can to some extent test the software they are developing to see if it is running correctly. And some of the software had been implemented already and was performing in a production environment. That's not to say that I was able to work as fast as usual. Concentrating was difficult, due to the levetiracetam I was taking. That medicine also made me tired. I remember once taking a scheduled dose right before a conference call. I decided to lay on the bed to take the conference call, as I sometimes do when working from home. That was a mistake. I woke up to the sound of music in my telephone as the conference call had ended. I had fallen asleep.

Work was also fairly stressful at times, and stress was not what my body needed during its recovery. I had been out of the development loop for several weeks, and now

I was being thrown back into projects where decisions and changes that I was unaware of had been made during that time. There were some early-morning (5AM) implementations that interfered with my sleep schedule occasionally. And having to complete projects with less resources in recent weeks had stressed everyone out, including my boss. For example, I remember one afternoon finishing changes to a software service that was to be implemented early the next morning. Having already worked extra hours on the previous implementation the day before, I stopped work at 4PM so I could walk to Subway for dinner. On my way back, I received a frantic call on my cell phone from my boss. A last-minute change was needed immediately with the service. My boss wanted me to log on immediately and make the change. I told him I was out walking and not by my computer, so I would not be able to make the change until later in the evening. He got upset. "Well if you can't make the change, I will find a developer who will!", he exclaimed. Then the line dropped. Had he hung up on me? I hoped the phone had not disconnected leaving him thinking I hung up on him.

My walking ability continued to improve. Within about a month, I was walking about 3 mph. Although my normal walking speed is around 4mph, 3mph is about an average walking speed. I was back to walking about 3 miles every evening, as well as at lunch. The only difference from normal is that my right leg still hurt too much to run. Therefore, I no longer ran across major streets when traffic was clear. Instead, I would now cross the street at stop lights. Besides the improved walking ability, the bruising on my right leg was also healing significantly. After about a month, I felt comfortable wearing short pants again while out walking. The leg was still tender, but no longer looked hideous.

During my first month home from the hospital, I was in remarkably good mental health, considering what I had been through. Although I had lost interest in the technical reading that normally occupied my time, I still enjoyed leisure activities such as listening to music, walking, and following weather and storms throughout the US. I enjoyed my free time on the weekends, and sometimes wished the weekends were longer. I was sleeping well. I was productive with my work. In retrospect, I think I must have at that point been in denial of what had happened. The first stage in a traumatic event or loss is often denial. Intellectually, I was well aware of the details of what had happened. I could talk about it intelligently. But emotionally, the serious events that had just happened, as well as the other issues I now faced in my life, had not yet sunk in. I think that the levetiracetam I was taking to prevent seizures was also acting as a tranquilizer, keeping some of the uncomfortable emotions buried. Because right as I finished tapering off the levetiracetam, the emotional issues began to grow. But that would not be until a month after I got out of the hospital.

THUNDERSTORM

Saturday, June 1. I had worked my first full week (well, not counting the Memorial Day holiday) from home. Now that things were settling down a bit, I got in touch with old friends from the past who had not yet heard about my brain aneurysm. I talked by phone with one old friend from Indiana about more details of my experience. Yet the emphasis was more on the fact that I was now rapidly getting well, and going back to my old interests and habits.

I enjoyed listening to music, and had just received a couple of CD albums I had bought to replace some worn-out music tapes. I enjoyed reading two books on storm chasing my boss had kindly sent me as a "get-well" gift when I got home from the hospital. And I had already build one microcontroller circuit since I had been home from the hospital.

In addition to the new circuit I had built in the past week, there was another circuit that I longed to test. In the time between my one and only storm chase, and my brain aneurysm, I had built another lightning detector. This detector used a commercial integrated circuit chip that can judge the distance to a storm, and is also good at rejecting false alarms from electrical noise. There had been no storms to test it since I had built it. But thunderstorms were predicted as possibility late that day. I was prepared – ready to monitor the circuits. And I was going to record on video how each of the lightning detectors I now had performed during any storm that occurred.

In the late afternoon, I was busy with reading when I noticed the sky growing dark outside. I checked the weather radar. Sure enough, some weak storms were developing to the west, moving this way. I began filming the sky and the indications on my lightning detectors. Eventually, the storm moved overhead. Thunder could be heard, and rain began falling. I filmed the storms, and how each detector reacted to their approach.

Before long, the storm was over. I began analyzing the data that the detectors had recorded. I edited the video footage I had filmed to show the performance of each of the lightning detectors. Having been helped by video reviews of products on YouTube, I wanted to post my evaluations of the storm detectors as well. Plus I wanted to upload a video with me speaking, so that my friends would know I was recovering nicely. I sent my friend in Indiana a link to the video as soon as I had uploaded it. Quickly I got a response back. "It's really you! You're back to normal!"

But besides the storm I had enjoyed that day, there were two other storms that I was blissfully unaware of. The first storm had happened the day before in Oklahoma. For the first time ever, storm chasers were killed – three of them. The group I had chased with twice previously also experienced close calls that would make me re-evaluate my own commitment to storm chasing.

The second storm was an emotional storm that was to batter my life in the coming months, and make me totally re-evaluate my values. Because apparently, at this point, I was still in shock from my close brush with death, and in denial of the life problems I now faced. I had gone back to life almost exactly as it was prior to my brain hemorrhage. Very little was different. Little did I know that it would be well over a year before I was again living a life that was anything close to normal, and how different my values would become from what they were presently.

STORM CHASER DEATHS

On Sunday June 2nd, I went to church as usual. I participated in the Bible Study afterwards, since there was no Sunday School for kids to teach in the summer. Sunday afternoons, I usually do errands, such as paying bills and doing cleaning. I did that. I took my usual evening walk. Then it was relaxation time. One thing I enjoyed doing during storm season was reading chase accounts by current storm chasers. Not only did I like watching the video they captured of the storms, but I also liked following the logic they used in making predictions for where to go on a chase.

On a chase discussion board I read regularly, I soon ran across a message thread entitled something like "Mike Bettes Hit By Tornado!". Mike Bettes was a storm chaser for the Weather Channel. I had met him briefly on a storm chase the previous year. I have an ap on my iPhone that shows the GPS location of storm chasers who share this information. I remember late one evening as our chase group had dinner in a restaurant, I saw another chaser who was very close to our location. The icon said

"Bettes". Since I do not subscribe to cable, and had not watched the Weather Channel in years, I did not know who Mike Bettes was. I asked our tour leader, if he knew someone named "Bettes". He said yes, that is Mike Bettes from the Weather Channel, but why did I ask? I showed him the icon on my screen. Apparently, Mike Bettes had made storm predictions for the next day that brought him to the same locations as our predictions brought us. Our tour leader thanked me for the information. Each of us on the tour met Mike briefly as we stopped to observe a developing storm.

While at the hospital, I had frequently watched the Weather Channel. I saw Mike Bettes being interviewed on some of his chases. The thought that crossed my mind is that he does take some significant risks by getting closer to tornadoes than most chasers would dare to. When I saw the message thread about him being hit by a tornado, my first thought was that it was someone's idea of a joke. But as I read through the thread and saw all the discussion, I realized that this was for real. A tinge of fear went through me. No chaser had ever been seriously injured by a tornado before in the history of storm chasing. And now, one had taken a direct hit by a tornado. Fortunately, I soon learned that he and his crew were okay, with only minor injuries from the incident.

I stopped to think. I had been at the same location as Bettes chasing a storm the year before. Maybe I was in more danger than I realized. Though luckily his injuries were minor, he could certainly have been killed, since his vehicle had been directly hit and thrown 200 yards by a strong tornado. Being just sensitized to the dangers of unlikely but serious happenings by my brain aneurysm, this was a scary thought. But as I thought of it some more, my concern lessened. I had seen his dramatic live close-up live video on The Weather Channel several weeks earlier. I rationalized that he is far more aggressive than I would ever be with storm chasing. Working for the Weather Channel, he needed to capture dramatic footage to attract viewers. It almost served him right in fact, I thought. When you take chances for the dramatic shot, eventually it catches up with you. He probably didn't have as much experience as other chasers, including the ones leading the tour I was on the previous year. And, even after all that, he still had not been seriously injured. If that's all that happened to him with the chances he takes, then I am safe with the smaller risks I'm willing to take. But right after I convinced myself of that, I read another thread. There were three other chasers who had been hit by the tornado as well. Tim Samaras, age 55, along with his son, Paul Samaras, age 24, and Carl Young, age 45, had not been so lucky. They were all killed. They were among the most experienced chasers in the field. And they were not ones to deliberately put themselves in danger for the sake of a dramatic shot. They were research scientists, with a philosophy very similar to mine. That was a scary thought. I stopped reading the forum and turned my thoughts to other, more pleasant, things.

At the church service I had attended on Sunday, the pastor had announced that they would be trying an experimental outdoor service on several Sundays during the summer. That did not affect me, because it was not the service I attend (the 8AM service). But one thing did catch my attention. He emphasized that the dress code for this service would be informal. "Go ahead and wear your short pants to these services – you will not be out of place!", he said. Although I had long since outgrown this, as a child and teenager I hated to dress up. I would do my best to not attend any place that required me to dress up. Wearing dress clothes to church or work was no longer a big deal to me, and I had no desire to come to church in shorts. But my father and I still debated frequently about the role of professional dress. For example, my father felt uncomfortable going to a doctor who wore casual clothes. He also often complained about the dress of others at the church he was presently attending, saying he saw it as disrespectful. I didn't care about dress. Here was another example of someone in a highly respected position who did not think dressing up was important. This would be something I could use as an "I told you so" with my father.

I normally talk to my father twice a week, on Tuesday evenings and Saturday mornings. I was excited about talking to him on Tuesday, because I would have a chance "score one". Having been somewhat beaten down by all the serious happenings related to my brain aneurysm, and the stress of returning to full-time work, this was something I was looking forward to. That evening, my father did not seem to be in a very good mood. His arthritis was bothering him. Nevertheless, I went on with my planned speech. "Pastor announced on Sunday that the church will be holding several outdoor services for the summer. Oh yes, and he said to be sure to wear SHORT PANTS to them!". My father was unamused. "I know you won't believe things like this", he said grimly "but there were three storm chasers killed on Friday. You might want to consider that when you think about chasing in the future. You're going to get yourself hurt or killed storm chasing." I replied that yes, I was aware that three chasers had died. But that this was the first time any chasers had ever been killed, and there were hundreds of chasers out there every year. The phone call soon concluded. But the chaser deaths were bothering me now.

I went online and did more reading about the chasers and their death. There was no denying it. These were experienced chasers and research scientists, not thrill-seekers by any means. I then decided to read the blog of one of the drivers from the team I had chased with the year before. Were they on this tornado as well? Did they have any close calls? What I read was an even bigger shock. Not only had they been chasing this same tornado, but they had a very close call with it. They became stuck in traffic in Oklahoma City as the tornado approached. Their only way to escape had been to drive north through the core of the heaviest rain and largest hail. Though no one had been injured, the tornado had at one point came within a couple of blocks of their location. A few seconds of difference might have meant their deaths as well. I was going to have to seriously reconsider if I wanted to chase in the future.

I continued to read more about the tornado online. Someone had posted a video of Mike Bettes's encounter with the tornado and his subsequent interview on YouTube. I watched it. The video that they filmed as their car was lifted by the tornado was scary, but it was about what I expected. But there was something profoundly scary about the interview afterwards. It brought me almost to a state of panic. I just couldn't figure out why that was. Was it the fact that Bettes said "When we were airborne, I thought maybe I was going to heaven." Was it a general fear of death, and a realization that I too had come close to death with my brain aneurysm? Maybe that was part of it, but it seemed that there was something beyond that. The interview was filmed outside a motel. There was a young cameraman who also described his experience riding with Bettes as their vehicle was hit by the tornado. There was something scary to that. There was something scary about Mike Bettes sitting there calmly in front of the motel doing the interview. I couldn't put my finger on it. I tried to put it out of my mind. I had things I needed to get done. But the image, particularly the young cameraman describing his experience, would not leave my mind. It seemed that every time images of that interview entered my mind, I would panic. But why? Okay, so maybe I shouldn't chase. The risks are relatively low (I later calculated the risk of death at, conservatively, about 1 in 10,000 per week of chasing). Even after I decided I wasn't going to chase anymore, there was something terrifying about the interview scene. This was my first hint of mental issues that would take control of my life later during the summer.

LAST WILL AND TESTAMENT

Due to the risk of seizures following brain surgery, and the anti-seizure medications I was taking which could impair my ability to drive, I was not allowed to drive for over a month after I got home from the hospital. I was fortunate enough to be able to work from home, so I was earning a paycheck. That was important, because expenses did not go away just because I was sick. In fact, they increased. New bills were arriving nearly every day – bills for ambulance services, diagnosis, hospital procedures, lab fees, and the like. At least once a week, I had followup appointments with various doctors. Some were not located close by. I spent as much as $110 in round-trip taxi fairs for one appointment. Fortunately, I've always been conservative financially. I have no debts, and save a sizable fraction of my income. I had been just about to make a $10,000 investment with funds that had accumulated in my checking account right at the time I had my brain aneurysm. As it turns out, $10,000 was about the amount I spent out-of-pocket for co-insurance payments and other medical expenses during the second half of the year. So although I didn't save any money during the rest of the year, I didn't have to tap into any savings funds.

My neurologist was having me gradually taper off the anti-seizure medicine levetiracetam. When I first got out of the hospital, I was taking two tablets four times a day, for a total of 8 tablets every day (400mg total). Every week, I would drop the amount slightly, per the orders from my neurologist. It is dangerous to abruptly stop anti-seizure medications. Doing so can actually cause seizures. At my follow-up appointments, my neurologist always asked if I was having any "issues" with discontinuing the anti-seizure medicine. I thought that was a strange question. Why would I be having "issues" doing it? I was happy to be gradually taking less medicine. One thing I didn't realize is that, though levetiracetam is used to control seizures, it also has a tranquillizing effect. Perhaps that helped to explain how I fell asleep on a conference call for work on day shortly after taking a dose. It might also explain why I was sleeping well – sometimes sleeping through the entire night or just waking up once (compared to my normal habit of waking up several times during the night). By the last week in June, I was down to taking just half a pill a day, at bedtime. At this point, my neurologist cleared me to drive again.

I knew I needed to take it easy with getting back into driving. I would not want my initial trips to be driving on the freeway in heavy commute-time traffic, and through the construction downtown Buffalo. So I continued to work from home for a while. My first trip would be just a couple of miles away, to have my car oil changed. An oil change was due around the time of my aneurysm, and it was now two months late. It had been two months since I had driven. Would my car even start? I turned the key on my 2008 Toyota Corolla. The engine cranked. It started right up, as if I had had never sat idle. Amazing! I put the car into reverse to back out of the parking space at my apartment, where my car had sat for the past two months. It didn't budge. I gave it a bit of gas. Still nothing. Finally, with a bit more gas, I heard a "clunk", and the car began moving backwards. The wheels had been frozen from sitting still for two months.

I drove uneventfully to the shop for an oil change. Driving still seemed familiar and not an issue, even though I had not driven in two months. A young guy, in his early 20's, serviced my car. Did I look like an old man now? Did he realize that the person he was talking to had almost died weeks earlier? The whole situation seemed surreal. For the first time, I felt old – and I realized my mortality. It hit me like a ton of bricks. While in the hospital, I had quickly learned the seriousness of my condition. I knew that there was roughly a one in three chance that I would die. Yet, it really didn't seem to worry me that much at the time. Of course, I wanted to live, and would do everything I could to pull through. But I was right with God, and if I had to die, I would accept that. At the hospital, instead of worrying that I might die, I kept my mind on other things, and on enjoying (as much as possible) the moment. I would listen to music and compose E-mails on my iPhone. I would keep up with weather conditions throughout the country and financial markets, because that was what I enjoyed doing. In retrospect, I was probably in the "shock" stage of my loss. Though I understood intellectually, it still had not hit me emotionally. Perhaps the levetiracetam acting as a tranquilizer also played a role. Now that I was nearly weaned from levetiracetam, thoughts about what I had just gone through terrified me.

Though I had not been particularly scared of dying from a mental standpoint during my hospital stay, one thing that had really bothered me was what would happen to my estate. I had saved up a pretty sizable amount of money since I began working more than 25 years earlier, but had never created a will. Since I had no brothers, sisters, or spouse, it was likely that the money would be divided up among various distant relatives who I didn't even know – with a large portion of it going to lawyers overseeing the process. The charities and research organizations I supported on a regular basis would receive nothing. I knew I needed to make a will soon. Now that I could drive to see a lawyer, it seemed like a reasonable time to do this. But making a will and related arrangements proved to be far more difficult and emotionally draining than I would have ever imagined.

I asked around church if anyone could recommend a lawyer to prepare a will. I was recommended a semi-retired lawyer who is a member of the congregation. I set up an appointment with him for Saturday, June 22.

In my now-sensitized emotional state, it felt not like I was planning for something in the distant future, but as if death was imminent for me soon. I dreaded facing the task of thinking about my will. But after working on Friday the 21st, that evening I sat down and faced the task. I looked at charities I regularly gave money to presently, as well as charities I had supported in the past. I brainstormed other organizations I would like to support but had never given to in the past. As I worked through this, I began to feel better. My concentration was no longer about the realities of my eventual death, but on solving the problem of dividing the estate. After a few hours, I was satisfied that I had a rough idea how I wanted to divide things. The lawyer would have the information he needed to formalize this.

Saturday morning I drove to see the lawyer in the next town. Being semi-retired, he had a tiny office. His wife served as his secretary. Though I had never met either one of them before, I found out that I had taught his grandson in Sunday School several years earlier. The notes I had made on how my estate should be divided seemed logical to him. But there were a couple of complications. First, I would need someone to be a medical care proxy for me in the event that I was unable to make decisions for myself. I was familiar with this concept due to my father, who had a living will. I assumed I could do the same. But unlike in Virginia where my father lives, New York law requires an actual person to be assigned to dictate my wishes. Simply documenting my wishes in a legal document would not be sufficient. Second, I would need an executor, someone to execute the will after my death. That need was part of the reason I had put off creating a will in the first place. I didn't know who I would burden with, or trust, with this duty. While I had co-workers and other acquaintances in Buffalo, none of them seemed appropriate for the responsibilities involved. A couple of long-time friends crossed my mind as appropriate, but they lived in other parts of the country. They would not be able to be my health care proxy. So I was faced with a dilemma. I would need to resolve this before I could go any further. Still, I felt good that I had taken the first step in my estate planning.

With the meeting with the lawyer out of the way for now, and the ability to drive again for the first time in two months, I was going to try to do something for pleasure for a change. That day, June 22, was Field Day, an emergency preparedness exercise participated in by thousands of ham radio operators throughout the country. It was being held at the local radio club's repeater site – the same site I had been scheduled to help with work at the day after my brain aneurysm. In past years, I had greatly enjoyed this activity. Besides a chance to get on the air and make contacts, it also provided a chance to socialize with others from the club. But I was a bit nervous about going on that day. I knew everyone else in the club would be asking me questions about my brain aneurysm, since this would be the first time I had been together with them since it happened. Wanting to put all the bad memories behind me as quickly as possible at this point, I was not wanting to have to re-tell my story multiple times to others. Normally, I might talk with others about what I had been recently doing with radio. But the trouble was – I had not been doing anything with radio recently. I had been too busy with hospitalization, work, and doctors appointments over the past two months to mess around with radio. The last major technical project I had worked on that people might be able to relate to was FreeSWITCH – which I worked on the evening I had my brain aneurysm. I had long since deleted that application, as just the thought of it made me sick due to its association with my brain aneurysm.

I arrived at the Field Day site during the early afternoon. By that time, the club had already finished setting up the radios and antennas, and it was time to begin making contacts (officially, contacts begin at 2PM Eastern time). There were three radios set up. Others from the club were already operating two of the radios. I sat down at the third radio. But it seemed something was wrong with the radio I was using. All the signals I was hearing were weak. And whenever I attempted to make a contact, the station on the other end could not hear me. Based on the symptoms, I suspected a problem with the antenna. Using a multimeter, I determined that the antenna was shorted. I inquired as to whether anyone else had been successful using the radio I was using. They had not been; I was the first one to use it. Another club member and I, proceeded to make other measurements to track down where the short was. Soon we were able to locate and resolve the issue. The other club member congratulated me on recognizing and tracking down the problem. I sat down at the radio and made a few contacts.

We each brought food, and we grilled a picnic dinner. Although a couple of people asked in general terms how I was doing, and one asked specifically about my leg when he saw that I was still walking with somewhat of a limp, I was pleasantly surprised that not everyone wanted me to repeat my medical story. As we ate, the young four-year-old son of one of the members ran around gleefully. Just like had been happening at field days for the past 15 years. One big thing was different now though. I realized that the father was not of my generation. I was old enough to be his father, not the father of the young boy. Though I regularly talked to this club member at past field days, I had never really thought about that before prior to my brush with mortality. Then there was the young professor who I always talked about physics with. He was planning to camp out at the Field Day site overnight, being used to outdoor activities of that type. I realized once again, for the first time, he was not my peer – but more like the age where he could have been my son.

After I took the last of the medicines related directly to my brain aneurysm on the evening of June 25, I decided it was time to put away all the hospital stuff and start moving on with my life. Displayed prominently in my living room was the Get Well poster the kids had me for me while I was in the hospital. At the table, there was my medical band from the hospital, at well as my hospital release papers, doctor appointment schedule details, get-well cards, and a detailed log of my medicine schedule over the past month. I put all of this away. The room looked strange, after looking at these things multiple times a day over the past month. Realizing now that levetiracetam also acts as a tranquilizer, I wondered if I would have trouble sleeping the night of the 26th. In fact, I did have a bit of trouble getting to sleep initially. But that was just for the first night. The following nights I slept okay. Little did I realize the hell of sleeplessness I would experience starting a month later.

Not sure who to look to for Power of Attorney and as executor of my will, I hoped to get some help from my church. I was, after all, planning to leave them a sizable portion of my estate. Perhaps the church itself could be listed as an executor? I set up an appointment to meet with the pastor to discuss this. That appointment was scheduled for morning of Tuesday July 2nd. Due to holiday schedules, that was the only day the pastor had any time to meet with me. Still working from home on that day, I stopped work mid-morning and walked to the church for my appointment. I was told the pastor had not gotten in yet. As I waited for him to arrive, I sat around thinking about my estate planning. Finally the pastor arrived, apologizing for being late. He commended me on my plans to leave the church a portion of my estate. He even agreed that he and the visitation pastor would play the role of Power of Attorney for me. But when I asked about making the church executor of the will he seemed very surprised. He had not heard of this being done before, and would need to check with the church's accounting department and possibly a lawyer. I left that day disappointed and frustrated, because I was still no further along with completing my will. However, the pastor promised that he would be getting back with me shortly.

A week later, I still had not heard from the pastor. The timing of the 4th of July holiday was unfortunate, because many people who might have answers were still out of town. After two weeks, I still had not heard anything, and so I talked to the pastor at church. He apologized for the delay and said I should be hearing from him the following week. But I still heard nothing. Late in the week, I E-mailed the pastor for an update. I got no response. I knew I would need to talk to him again at church on Sunday. But when I got to church Sunday, I found out that the pastor had now gone out of town to a leadership convention. The assistant pastor knew nothing of his progress regarding my will.

Having estate arrangements constantly hanging over my head was not helping my anxiety. And it no longer seemed that my church would be the solution. I would have to think of something else. I did have two long-time friends who I felt I could trust handling the affairs of my estate. They could not have power of attorney, since they lived in other states, but presumably they could be executor for my will. One of my friends I had known since elementary school. We grew up together, and still kept in touch. Another friend who I trusted had worked with me at an earlier job in Buffalo, but had since moved to Chicago. I E-mailed both friends, saying I had an important matter that I wanted to talk with them about by phone. I talked with both friends, and they both agreed to be executor for my will. Since my friend in Chicago is nearly 10 years younger than me, I thought he would be the best one to list as primary executor. My other friend in Virginia, who I had grown up with, would be secondary executor. They both agreed to this.

But there was still one more major issue to be resolved before I could complete my will. Per the lawyer, I needed to create a list of close relatives, even if they were not to be heirs. If this was not done, there could be legal issues at the time of my death. Although I had not remained particularly close with relatives on my mother's side as an adult, I at least knew who they all were and could provide their current locations. My father's side was a bigger problem. With the exception of his brother, who had already died, my father had not kept up with any of his relatives as an adult. He did not know which ones were still alive, or where they might be living. After talking with the lawyer again, we determined that I just had to make a "best effort" to find the information, in order to avoid problems with the estate at the time of my death. Listing the specific locations of relatives on my mother's side, and the last known location of those on my father's side (many of whom were likely already dead due to the age they would be) would be sufficient.

Finally, on the weekend of July 26, I had an official Last Will and Testament document. I sent copies to the two executors. I informed my pastor that although I would still be leaving a sizable portion of my estate to the church, I would not need the church to serve as an executor. He apologized for not having gotten back to me, citing hectic schedules. I was glad I no longer had this gruesome task hanging over my head.

INDEPENDENCE DAY

Now cleared to drive, I began driving to work again the first week of July. I decided to take it slow. I would drive to work two days and work from home the rest of the days the first week. I would add a day of driving in to work in each of the next three weeks, until I was driving into work on all days. Of course, I still had frequent doctors appointments – averaging one per week or more. On those days I would need to continue working from home so I could drive to the appointment from home at whatever time is occurred during the day. Most of my appointments were in Orchard Park, which meant just a few mile drive from home. Work is more than 15 miles away in Buffalo, so a drive from there could add 30 miles to the trip. Working some days from at home also gave me more time to relax and sleep, since I saved about an hour that I would normally spend commuting. I was still sleeping 8 to 9 hours a night at this point, and was spending considerable time walking each day.

In a way, it was good to be back at work. It certainly was an accomplishment after all the physical issues associated with my surgery. I was also starting to get lonely staying at home all the time. Although I did interact with others from work through frequent E-mails and conference calls, there was no casual conversation. As a geek and loaner, the majority of my social interaction was at work. However, I did find driving in to work to be a bit stressful. Downtown Buffalo was expanding rapidly due to a huge amount of development for the new University of Buffalo medical campus, and major reconstruction of the main downtown pedestrian area. That meant many road closures and delays. On several evenings when leaving from work, I got lost on the detours and ended up on the Skyway – instead of Route 190 – trying to get out of Buffalo. This meant a longer commute with worse traffic to add to the stress. At lunchtime, my daily 45 minute walk downtown was now filled with loud jack hammers, closed sidewalks, and crowding as pedestrians were squeezed onto the few remaining open streets and sidewalks. At work, I was also having trouble getting involved in social conversations. I have always been somewhat of a loaner, but tend to work on quite a few hobbies and other interests at home which others are interested in. But now, my focus was on just dealing with medical issues and trying to get caught up with things from work. I didn't want to burden others with these personal problems. In addition, there was a lot of negativity in the office at that time. Already feeling somewhat anxious and depressed, I did my best to avoid others when they were being negative. And with the strong economy, there were a ton of projects being worked on simultaneously, which meant none of us really

too fast of a pace. I was able to consume enough calories at the expense of quality by eating more sweets, such as orange juice and ice cream. Sometimes I would even enjoy eating those things. But in general, eating meals was a chore with my lack of appetite.

I also found my interests and ability to concentrate diminishing. When I first got home from the hospital, I had already done a couple of small electronic projects. Now the thought of doing any kind of project seemed oppressive. On the July 4th holiday, I knew I should try to focus on a project for fun, to start developing my interests again and get my mind off my problems. I had bought a Raspberry Pie computer months earlier, prior to my aneurysm, but had always been too busy to set it up. I thought this would be a good thing to work on, now that I had the time. Plus, one of my office mates had an interest in this device as well. Perhaps that would give me something to talk about socially. But as I worked to get this set up, the task seemed never-ending. The normal problems encountered during setting this up, which normally would have been a fun challenge, seemed to be insurmountable obstacles. I felt burnt out. After some hours of slow progress, I did in fact manage to get things all set up. But I felt no sense of accomplishment, and no desire to play with the device once it was set up. It ended up sitting around unused for few weeks, after which I got tired of looking at it and put it away.

Feeling lonely and discouraged that evening, I decided I needed to get out into a social situation. There was the annual Independence Day parade and fireworks a mile or so from where I lived. I never attended this in the past, but tonight I would go. I carried a small folding chair as I walked the mile or so to the parade route. I sat and watched the parade. The last time I had seen a parade was over a decade earlier, when I had helped provide radio communications for a parade in a nearby town where I had lived at the time. Tonight, it felt like I had no purpose for being at the parade. Just to sit and watch, which was not that enjoyable.

After the parade, I walked with my chair to the town pavilion, where the fireworks were to be displayed. I noticed people setting their chairs very near the grassy area where the fireworks would be launched from. "That's too close for comfort.", I thought. I wanted a good view of the fireworks, but wanted to be far enough away to not be hit by any falling debris from the fireworks. So I set up my chair a block or so back from the field. As it turned out though, I was not back far enough. Suddenly in the middle of the fireworks display, I felt a sharp pain in my left leg. It felt like I had just been hit with a large rock. "Ouch!", I exclaimed, as I jumped up from my chair. I didn't know what had happened. At first, I thought maybe some kids were throwing rocks into the air, and I had been hit by one. But apparently, it was a left-over piece from a firework that had not fully detonated. Fortunately, it was my left leg that was hit – as my right leg was still sore from the operation. In coming days, I had bruising on both legs – the remaining bruising from the operation on my right leg, and the bruise from being hit by the firework on my left leg. As far as I am aware of, no one else – including those sitting much closer to the display – got hit that night.

I walked home from the fireworks display. I forced myself to eat an evening snack to get my daily calories up to 1200. Then I went to bed. The following day, Friday, would be a regular work day for me. Just about everyone else at the office was taking the day off, but I had no remaining vacation time due to having to take all my sick and vacation time for my brain aneurysm. Not that I would have enjoyed another day off anyway at that point.

WELCOME TO OLD AGE

I was 48 years old when my brain aneurysm ruptured. I never felt like an "old man" before that.

All my life, I heard people lamenting getting older. As a teen, I remember laughing at a joke about a "40 year old ass". Even teens lamented the loss of the "good old days" of childhood, and that made perfect sense to me as a teen. By early adulthood though, such things no longer made sense to me or caught my attention. I tried to learn what I could from people of all ages – be they young children, people my age, or senior citizens such as grandparents. And I was happy to be creating my own life using what I learned, with little desire to be any other age. I remember my parents, as well as my friends, made a big deal about what a milestone it was when I turned 30. I was not impressed. I was happy to be 30. I never was able to identify very well with the lifestyles of "20-somethings". The drinking, partying, taking risks and poor care of the body that seemed to typify many of my contemporaries was repulsive to me. The 30s were an age where people concentrated on their career and on raising a family. With all my computer and other technical interests, I could certainly identify with interest in a career. I enjoyed keeping up with the latest technology and scientific advances made by my peers. And I enjoyed working with kids, so I would be able to relate to parenting as well.

The day I turned 40 (in 2004), I was unexpectedly laid off from my job. Lining up a new job kept my mind busy then, and fortunately only took a couple days. Being 40, did realize that the joke about the "40 year old ass" now applied to me. That was a bit disconcerting, but not a big deal. Okay, so I was now too old to ever have a family, but that was never one of my big goals anyway. I enjoyed working with kids, but only certain ages. I never did think I would be able to be a good parent when it came to dealing with say babies or teenagers. I "got my fill" of interacting with kids by teaching Sunday School for my church, and playing with friends' kids. Likewise, the fact that I had turned 40 would not really have much of an effect on my career and technical interests. True, I probably couldn't learn as fast as someone in their 20's, but I could still learn all the new things I was interested in, as well as new things required by my work. And almost all of my time at home was spent doing technical things with radio or science. That was not going to change just because I turned 40. Throughout my 40s (prior to my brain aneurysm), I never paid much attention to my age. Most of my co-workers were 10 to 15 years younger than me, and I related to them just fine.

One year as I began teaching a new Sunday School class, one of the other teachers made a comment about how we were now older than typical parents of the children we were teaching. My response to that was something like "True – but why do we care? Most of the teachers are also female, and we are male, but so, what difference does any of that make?" I was well aware that I was getting older, but the only difference it really made was that I knew I had less years left of life, and that meant I needed to concentrate more on what was important to me. There was no great sense of loss in this.

A couple months after my hospital stay, in retrospect I see that I began suffering from PTSD. This was no doubt caused by the physical and psychological stress of my brain aneurysm and subsequent life changes. One effect of PTSD is that it makes one hypervigilant and very aware of anything negative. In retrospect, I see that this hypervigilance led me to far overestimate the impact of now being an "old man".

At first, I didn't know what was bothering me as I saw younger people. But it became apparent during the month of July. One day I was in a grocery store looking for something when a younger guy, probably around 30, struck up a conversation with me regarding a product we were buying. We began discussing nutrition. I had always seen myself in similar conversations as a young scholar, who has done his research on all sorts of health issues and was happy to provide advice to "elders" who asked. But I now suddenly saw myself instead as an "old man", who has to be very careful about what he eats out of fear of cholesterol levels and heart attack risks. I felt this guy probably saw me as some boring old man, and was glad to get away from such a bore.

For a decade or more, I had spent all my free time on learning, technical interests, and experimenting with electronics and computers. I never went to social events. Those old technical interests now felt meaningless. What little social involvement I did have often consisted of talking about technology or science. Now I didn't have even those interests, and my thoughts were also being slowed down and confused by the strong emotions which I now realize were associated with my developing PTSD. With time no longer being taken up by technical interests, as well as developing anxiety and depression related to PTSD, I often felt lonely. So even though I had little to contribute, I forced myself to go to social events. I forced myself to make small talk at the church picnic, but it felt very odd, and added to my stress level. It also emphasized, again, the fact that I was older than the majority of the people there.

One day during the fall when I was visiting my psychologist (who was treating my PTSD and other psychological symptoms), I began noticing other patients in the waiting room. While at doctor offices in the past, I never paid much attention to others – always being busy reading something. But this time I noticed a couple of things. First, most of the patients were female. In my state of PTSD, where every little negative seemed to be a crisis, I felt inferior. Here I'm "supposed" to be a strong guy, but I'm in with all the "weak" gals. A much bigger issue I noticed though was all the other patients were significantly younger than me. They had most of their life ahead of them to solve their problems. I no longer did. That thought sent me into almost a panic on the spot. It took hours to begin to feel a small amount of relief from the anxiety after that.

Another "feature" of old age is the task of dealing with aging parents in declining health. My mother had died much earlier, when I was 33. While obviously a very sad event in my life, I realized that this death was untimely as far as its place in my life. As a young adult, I was very involved in my career and hobbies and was thus able to keep my mind off the loss. I would think of it particularly when I talked to my father on the phone, but even then I was handling it much better than he was, and I took a sense of accomplishment at being able to cheer my father up, provide advice, and eventually get him interested in other things. Now in the past couple years, my father's health had also been deteriorating. Arthritis was severely impacting his ability to get around. I didn't really think about it much when I talked to him on the phone, because he rarely complained of the arthritis and always sounded like his "old self" over the phone. But I had found myself feeling depressed over his deterioration when I visited him in person in recent years.

With the negative bias set by PTSD, and with my father now beginning to complain about his loss of abilities, the situation became prominent in my mind. I felt like I needed to visit my father. But I could not. Late in the winter, I had made arrangements to visit my father during the spring. The week I was scheduled to visit turned out to be the week after I had my aneurysm. I spent that time in the hospital. I used all my vacation and sick time for my hospitalization and subsequent doctor appointments. Even if I had been able to take unpaid time off, I still could not visit my father. For one thing, any impending event caused my not to be able to sleep at all the night before. My only task was to survive my work and make it to the next day, not be concerned with taking time off for a vacation. And my father did not want me visiting him. He has always had a great concern that something would happen to me while visiting him. For example, he would never allow me to drive when visiting him, insisting that I fly (the distance is around 800 miles). "If something happened to you while you were driving to visit me, I could never live that down", he would always say. Now he said he didn't want me visiting for "at least a year", concerned that something might happen with my brain aneurysm while I was traveling to visit him. So here was my father, deteriorating in health I didn't know for sure how much, and I had not seen him in over a year. But for multiple reasons I could not visit him. I felt trapped.

Although, as a general rule, I seldom felt the need to discuss personal problems or ask for advice from my father in recent years, the fact was still that he was always there for me should I need to discuss something. Now I realized that this would not be the case for much longer. I realized when my mom died that this had happened unusually early. My father was in his mid-60s at the time. I knew my father was likely to be around for quite a bit longer, so I never really worried about that. But now he was past 80. His health was deteriorating. He was practically the only person of his generation who I was still close to and who was still alive. Since adulthood, I had never been real close with other relatives. Two adult neighbors from my childhood, as well as several friends of my father who I had been fairly close with, had all died within the past year. I valued talking to and getting input from a parental figure when I had problems. But I would likely not be able to get this much longer.

Probably the biggest symptom of advancing age is an increase in medical problems. Although I was no stranger to doctors, having suffered from thyroid issues as well as occasional issues with anxiety and depression for most of my life, now I had to be concerned about things I never really had to be concerned about before. Things like stroke and heart attack. And I had just had a very serious stroke (a brain aneurysm is considered a stroke), so indeed this was "baptism by fire" as my introduction to advancing age.

So this is the situation I found myself in during the summer of 2013. Suddenly I realize my life is 2/3 over (I realized that all along, but it never had bothered me before). It might even be a lot more than that over since I now have a serious medical condition. With that much of my life over, I might under ordinary circumstances use that as motivation to re-double my efforts to accomplish life goals. But my anxiety and PTSD are preventing me from taking such action. Intellectual an technical things I have taken so much pleasure in for the majority of my adult life now seem meaningless, and even if they seemed meaningful would be difficult to do in my emotional state. I've never been a real social person anyway, but now that I no longer have the technical interests I often talked with friends before, my friends are falling by the wayside. My father, who has been there all my life when things got tough, now instead needs support from me. Others of his generation that I was close to have all recently died. I'm now old enough to start having medical concerns that I never had to worry about in the past – and indeed that is happening with a "baptism by fire" with my brain aneurysm and subsequent symptoms.

THIS IS YOUR STORM

During July, I began having trouble sleeping on some nights. It seemed like if I didn't deliberately relax and take it easy for up to a couple of hours prior to bedtime (which was 10PM at the time), I would have trouble sleeping. For example, on the evening of July 17th, I got a call from a friend who I had asked to be executor for my will. He agreed to do it. We talked about his work and my recent experiences with my aneurysm. Although I enjoyed the conversation, it ended up lasting until 9:30. My over-sensitive nervous system was still revved up from this, and it took hours to fall asleep.

Friday July 19th had been a fairly good day for me. While my appetite was still low, I had felt somewhat less anxious and depressed. I made good progress on projects at work that day. That evening, storms began occurring nearby. And I was glad. I still needed to do some more testing and calibration on my lightning detectors. Though there had been some storms about 30 miles away, which allowed me to perform a bit more testing, there had not been any storms in the immediate area since the one on June 1st. Finally, this was "my storm".

As the sun set, I sat on my patio watching distant lightning. As I was doing this, I recalled how I used to sit waiting for storms at my home while growing up. Though I had done storm chasing, and I would now watch and monitor storms as they occurred at home, this was the first time in years I had sat on my patio just casually watching lightning. I had always been too busy to stop and just enjoy watching lightning from my patio. As I was watching though, negative thoughts began to fill my sensitized mind. I realized that years of studying storms had removed most of their mystery for me. Ordinary storms were no longer the big thrill and curiosity they were for me during my childhood and younger adulthood. Worse, sitting on my patio for the first time in years reminded me of how much of my life was now passed. I was no longer watching as a kid, or a young man. I was now an old man. The image of an old man, with nothing to do but sit on a rocking chair and watch the weather, flashed through my mind. Of course logically, I realized I wasn't *that* old yet, but I just couldn't seem to get that image out of my mind. I tried to run from it – it felt almost like a phobia. Not only did I feel like an old man, but an old man with serious mental issues – which I wasn't sure would be going away soon, if ever.

Around 9:45PM, the storm appeared to be mostly over. It had missed the immediate area, producing only light rain and a bit of distant thunder. I went back inside and began preparing for bed. As I brushed my teeth, I heard a beep from one of my storm detectors. "That must have been a closer strike from the back of the storm that just passed", I thought. Then I heard another beep. Within a few minutes, I was hearing a beep every few seconds. I pulled up the weather radar on my cell phone. Sure enough, there was a new storm developing just to the west – and it was headed directly for my location. It was now around 10PM. Pouring rain began. Frequent flashes of lightning illuminated the sky. With the constant beeping, I decided to turn off my storm alarm so as not to annoy my neighbors. This was the first time I had needed to do that.

At 10:30PM, the storm was still raging. Pouring rain. Strong winds. Frequent lightning strikes with loud thunder. While I was glad to be witnessing this storm, I began to become concerned for my sleep that night. I knew I didn't dare go to bed until the storm was over. But it continued on. Just after 11PM, things seemed to calm down. But a quick check of the radar showed still more activity approaching from the west. It soon arrived. I realized my sleep was going to be in trouble that night. Finally, at around midnight, the storms subsided. Radar indicated only light rain behind the storms. I could finally go to bed.

I laid in bed, but could not fall asleep. 12:30AM. 1AM. 1:30AM. Finally, I must have fallen asleep, because I got woke up by a clap of thunder around 3AM. I laid in bed, listening to more rain. I could not go back to sleep again.

The rain ended, but I just laid there, unable to sleep until time to get up (then around 7AM). I had slept less than an hour the whole night.

My father called at his usual 7:30AM Saturday time. I was distraught. I described my insomnia of the previous night. When he asked my plans for the day, I really didn't know. I said I needed to get groceries, but after that I might not feel like doing anything other than taking a nap. I felt depressed and anxious. My father's reaction did not help my frame of mind. He said something like "Well, there's nothing wrong with not feeling good and needing to nap. As you get older, you'll see that more and more." I know my father can tend to be negative sometimes, and I do know not to take him seriously about things like this, but my sensitized, suggestible mind locked onto this negative thought. Just another example of the trials of getting older.

Although I slept better the following night, my overall sleep continued to worsen. Most nights I would lay awake for at least a few hours of the night – either when first trying to go to sleep, in the middle of the night, or later towards morning. My mental sensitization continued to worsen. Problems that would normally be "nothing at all" began to feel terrifying.

For example, on Monday the 22nd, as I drove to work, I began hearing a loud rattling, clanging sound from my car. I had just had the muffler replaced during an inspection the week before, so I was pretty sure it had to do with that. When I got to work, I checked the muffler, and it did not appear loose. I forgot about the noise until I heard it again many times while driving home from work. I started having an irrational fear of my car breaking down and leaving me stranded in the middle of a busy highway. Logically, I knew this fear was unfounded. In the worst possible scenario, the muffler might come loose – but that would not leave me stranded. Yet worries like this kept popping into my mind, causing my heart to race. When I got home, I was able to locate a panel that had came loose and was missing on screw. I knew I just needed to go back to the shop and have it taken care of. But when? In my sensitized state, I was totally exhausted, and could not bear the thought of going to the shop and possibly having to argue with someone to have it fixed. It was all I could do to get through the day at work, then come home and take a walk before beginning relaxing hours before bedtime. Something as simple as having this fixed seemed a formidable problem and stressor.

I waited until the next day, then called the auto shop from work and explained the problem. I arranged to take off work an hour early to have the problem fixed. The problem was fixed with no issue, and without any charge. Yet this simple repair act had seemed incredibly stressful. As I waited in the shop for my car to be fixed, a TV was on there. I never watch TV on my own. I saw some young contestants participating in some sort of a quiz show. The first thought that popped into my mind was once again that I was an "old man", and how lucky those contestants were to be young. A sense of panic overtook me, and I tried to push such thoughts away. Clearly my mind was exaggerating things, and making every minor negative thought seem like a crisis. Then getting home (now later than usual) and not being able to find a close place to park. Would I remember where I had left my car come morning?

As I drove home from work on Wednesday the 24th, I discovered the street I live on was closed for the evening for an annual festival. This happens every year. But this year, the simple act of having to park a couple of blocks away at a nearby shopping center and walk home felt like a crisis. I had horrible thoughts of forgetting where I had parked my car (my mind felt fried from the recent lack of sleep), or having it stolen. Again, I knew logically that my fears were unfounded, but this did nothing to allay my fears.

With the continued problems with sleep, appetite, and anxiety, I began to start researching what might be wrong with me. I was pretty sure the problem was not brain damage from the aneurysm itself, since the symptoms had not started until over two months after the aneurysm. Subsequent MRI scans and other checkups for the aneurysm revealed that everything was healing normally. I discussed my symptoms with my neurologist, be he was little help. He said these kind of symptoms "sometimes" occur after a brain aneurysm, and they can be either due to the trauma to the brain or to psychological factors (such as PTSD). Sometimes the symptoms are delayed, as in my case. Sometimes the symptoms eventually go away. That response was not helpful for me. I knew I was going to need to solve this problem on my own.

I had been on a wide variety of medicines after my surgery. But now I was back to the same medicines I had been taking all along. Or was I? I recalled that the hospital had replaced the statin I was taking to lower my cholesterol with a new one, and my doctor had subsequently changed my statin prescription accordingly as well. I checked the bottle. I was taking 60mg of atorvastatin daily. I looked up information on this drug. I found that 60mg was the highest possible dose. Furthermore, I found out that a sizable number of people experience issues when taking statins, especially when taken in high doses. Symptoms included, among others, loss of appetite, and even insomnia and anxiety! Further research showed that too low of a cholesterol level can actually be quite harmful. I logged onto my my doctor's web site and reviewed the results of the cholesterol test I had been given a few weeks after I got out of the hospital. He said the results were "good", so I hadn't paid much attention to them. It turned out that my total cholesterol (HDL and LDL combined) was just 99! Many people online with cholesterol levels this low reported mental issues. Apparently, cholesterol is necessary to synthesize neurotransmitters in the brain, and if it falls to low, brain functioning suffers.

Gleeful that I might actually have found the cause of the issues I was experiencing, I wrote a note to my doctor.

I explained the worsening symptoms of low appetite, insomnia, and anxiety, and what I had found in my research on possible dangers of too low of a cholesterol level. I asked if it would be possible for me to stop taking the atorvastatin, since my cholesterol level was very good in the last test and I was now eating a very healthy diet. My doctor's response was somewhat amusing. It went something like this:

What do you mean by "stop taking" atorvastatin? Of course you can't "stop taking" it. You had a stroke, remember? You will never be able to stop taking it. That said, not everyone tolerates high doses of statins well. I think it is reasonable to try a lower dosage. I am going to write you a prescription for a lower dose of atorvastatin, and we will continue to monitor your cholesterol levels on that does. The dose I am prescribing is 10mg.

So that was great! My doctor was now prescribing an atorvastatin dose of just 1/6 that I was previously taking (10mg vs 60mg). While I was still a bit nervous about taking a statin in general given the negative things I had read about them in my research, I realized that this change should certainly be enough for me to tell a big difference. Then if there was a big difference, I could take things from there and maybe switch to a different statin. At least I should be able to see some progress. I walked to the pharmacy and picked up the new prescription immediately after work.

BUDDY CHRIST, BUTTERMILK CREEK, FRACKING, AND THE PUKING PASTOR

I slept much better for the first week or two after lowering the atorvastatin dosage. Though not great, my appetite was also better than it was before. However, I still felt anxious and depressed much of the time during the day. I did have an occasional day where I felt (particularly during the afternoon and evening) pretty much like my "old self", becoming interested in various technical reading and even small projects. But these improvements would never last. No matter how hard I tried the next day to continue to stay involved and interested in what had held my attention the day before, the anxiety and depression would be back, and continuing to make effort on these things would become almost unbearable.

Seeing the improvement that had occurred with sleep and appetite after the statin dose reduction, I began to research statins to learn about their side effects in more detail. There was no shortage of information available, both online and through books. Of particular interest to me was that though statins reduce the risk of death due to heart attack, they can increase the risk other serious diseases such as diabetes[3]. There were also anecdotal reports of depression and memory loss. So although high doses of atorvastatin did decrease the risk of death from heart attack and stroke, the mental deficits they apparently cause led to enough more accidents that the overall death rate increased for high doses. Statins were known to have side effects on both sleep and mood, but most doctors considered these effects to be very rare. However, several respected physicians disagreed, even attributing severe episodic amnesia to statins[4].

One thing I saw consistently in the literature, though still speculative, was that statins reduce the amount of an enzyme known as COQ10 in the body. This enzyme is used by cells as part of the metabolic process, and it naturally decreases in the body as one grows older. There was talk that taking a COQ10 supplement could help counteract this issue. I researched the most reputable brands for this supplement, ordered some online, and began taking it each morning. As I began taking it each morning, it did seem energizing, and seemed to lift my mood slightly as well.

Yet during this time, I was starting to develop what might almost be considered a phobia – not of any particular

---

[3]   Top Cardiologist Argues We Should Dial Back On Statins Because Of Diabetes Risk, Forbes, March 4, 2012, http://www.forbes.com/sites/matthewherper/2012/03/04/top-cardiologist-argues-we-should-dial-back-on-statins-because-of-diabetes-risk/.

[4]   See book by Graveline, Duane, M.D. in Bibliography.

physical place, but of negative talk. From past experience with anxiety and depression (which I had suffered on and off with since childhood, most recently 12 years earlier in 2001), I realized I needed to maintain routines, keep my thoughts positive, and avoid negative topics or people. Unfortunately, my efforts to do this in my sensitized state ultimately resulted in my becoming actively fearful of the situations, sometimes to the point of near panic when they occurred.

My desk at work was located just a few feet from several co-workers, with no cubicles to help attenuate sound. All of these co-workers were younger than me, ranging from 15 years younger to just a few years younger. They would often engage in discussions about how horrible things were going in the world, how we as a society were doomed, etc. When this would happen, I would go to the restroom and sit for a while whenever possible. But I couldn't stay there indefinitely, as I needed to do my work. I also didn't feel that I should approach these co-workers about their conversations. Particularly with the accommodations that had been made for me in terms of being allowed to make liberal use of sick time and working from home, I didn't feel I was entitled to tell others how to do their work. Perhaps in retrospect I should have said something, or asked earlier to have my desk moved, but I also didn't want to admit (to myself or others) how much difficulty I was still having. So I would alternate between clumsy efforts to escape (to the restroom or arranging to get involved in meetings away from my desk), and suffering in silence. Some days were okay, with the negative conversations never occurring, particularly when co-workers needed to work from home. Other days things might be going relatively smoothly for me throughout the morning and early afternoon, only to have my spirits dashed and concentration ability shot when the negative conversations started up later in the afternoon. It seemed there was no end to the negativity I witnessed. There were three people in particular – Deklyn, Oliver, and Jimbo, who seemed to synergise and re-enforce each other when it came to negativity. They often hung out at Oliver's desk, just a few feet from my desk.

Deklyn was a younger co-worker who had recently married a highly religious girlfriend from a conservative state. Because of hearing so much about religion from his wife, Deklyn had begun to rebel against religion. One way he did this was by making use of the a gag figure called "Buddy Christ". Apparently this figure was a prop in movie from years earlier that had satirized the Catholic religion. After the movie, the prop was actually produced and sold by companies such as Amazon, so Deklyn had bought one and had it sitting on his desk. He would refer to it throughout the day. If he was having a discussion with someone visiting his desk about how to proceed with a given work project, he would pull out the figure and laugh loudly "So I wonder what Buddy Christ thinks we should do about this? What would he do? Repent, ye of little faith...." Likewise, when coding software, he would place Buddy Christ in a prominent position on his desk and say thinks like "Man, this is pure faith-based programming!" This seems pretty trivial, and I know he had been doing this for quite a while previously, but in my sensitized state it really bothered me. I didn't like the religion that was important to me being satirized, and I was sure he was a bad influence on my mannerisms. But in my state of anxiety, depression, and feeling inferior to others due to my health conditions, I didn't feel comfortable approaching him about it. I even talked with one of my pastors at church, and he agreed it would be best to just ignore the behavior for now.

Then there was Oliver, an avid outdoor enthusiast who spent much of his weekend time hiking and kayaking in nature preserves. Apparently he had recently run across rumors about a nearby stream, Buttermilk Creek, being contaminated by radioactive waste buried nearby. He would constantly talk about this, and his activism efforts to make people aware of the situation. Likewise, Jimbo had recently become convinced that the process of "fracking" (hydro-fracturing rocks to release stored natural gas and oil) was causing irreparable damage to the environment. He was constantly talking about how this practice doomed humanity.

But the most disturbing discussions were about the "puking pastor", who was a neighbor of Oliver. Oliver had had a run-in with a neighbor, who he knew was the pastor of a nearby church. When he looked up information about this church online, he found out that the pastor sometimes leads congregation members in a "sin purging" procedure that involves coughing and vomiting. It seems Oliver always found a way to bring this disgusting topic into his conversations. As an example, once Jimbo for some reason has started everyone discussing nuclear war (really pleasant topic to overhear thoughts on when in a sensitized state). During the discussion, he asked the question "So who should have the right to determine that all life on the earth gets extinguished? Should it be governments?" DJ chimed in with "Maybe Buddy Christ here should have that authority....". Then Oliver chimed in with "Oh, yes! I know who should have that right! It should be the Puking Pastor....."

My boss was too busy to notice any of these conversations, and even if he had he would not likely have said anything. His belief was that as long as people accomplished their work, it was none of his business how they acted. As a result of my anxiety and depression, I was too scared to take action to address the situation directly either by confronting my office mates or bringing it up to my boss. All I could do was hope that the situation would eventually improve, or that it would bother me less once my mental health began to improve. Actually, I did take one small action, though it was just a drop in the bucket of all the ongoing negative conversations. As a science geek, I knew that if there really was radiation at Buttermilk Creek, the media would have long since been hot on that trail, and everyone would know it. Also, in years past, I had done experiments involving radioactivity, and I still had a Geiger counter. So, after carefully thinking over what I was going to say, I got the nerve to approach Oliver one afternoon during his conversations about radioactivity in Buttermilk Creek. I told him that I had a Geiger counter he could borrow, so he could measure the radioactivity himself. This could help him in his activism, by providing actual radiation figures. Unfortunately, my Geiger counter was old and would only run using a DOS PC, which neither of us had anymore. However, Oliver did like the idea, and decided he would buy his own Geiger counter. I assisted him with picking one out. He ultimately did purchase a Geiger counter and take it to Buttermilk Creek. When he found no unusual radiation, he gradually stopped talking about the topic.

My concern with the above conversations probably seems really childish. Of course co-workers are going to talk about certain things. That is their business. Prior to my brain aneurysm, I would have been able to ignore it with little trouble, or if not then would have confronted the people involved. But in the state I was in, I chose to "run from" the problem, much like a person with a phobia runs from what they are scared of. In retrospect, I see that, like for the phobic, running from the problem provides short-term relief, but increases anxiety in the long term. A psychologist I was seeing for my issues later helped clarify this in my mind. When I described the negativity of my office mates, and how I was trying to escape its effects by running from it, he said something which has been very helpful to me. "Frank", he said, "Your mental health is not balanced on the head of a pin!" Meaning that yes – these situations are negative.

But they would have only minimal impact if it was not for the fact that I was building up anxiety and fear of them by running away from them each time. By going forward despite the discomfort, and not attempting to run away from the situations I feared, I was eventually able to (mostly) desensitize myself from my fears.

GUESS I WON'T BE TEACHING SUNDAY SCHOOL

Although I slept better in the days immediately following the atorvastatin dosage decrease, sleep problems returned shortly thereafter. For example, the night of August 7th I found myself awake and unable to sleep for several hours during the night. Other nights I slept okay, but during the day I continued to have problems with anxiety and depression. It seemed like if any major task was impending, it would adversely affect my sleep. For example, if I had to get up early for a work implementation at 5AM, I would find myself waking up at say 2AM and not being able to get to sleep again. Yet sometimes I would have difficulty sleeping even when nothing important was pending. Such was the case on Saturday night August 17th. I had just relaxed and done easy reading on Saturday. On Sunday nothing too important or unusual was pending – just going to church and the usual Sunday afternoon tasks of paying bills, cleaning, etc. Yet I still laid awake for hours on Saturday night. I was not really worrying or thinking negative thoughts – it was just that sleep would not come.

On Sunday the 18th, I felt very poorly. I was exhausted from having been awake much of the night, and I was feeling anxious and depressed. I attended church as usual. During the afternoon, I received a call from my elderly father. He had an idea for me – he thought I should get a Masters degree in engineering. In recent years, I had grown somewhat frustrated with my work in IT. I had graduated college with a B.S. in engineering, but had always worked in the IT field. Back in 2010, I had studied for and passed my EIT – an engineering exam that is the first step in being certified as a professional engineer. But I had not done anything beyond that. Though I had kept my father informed in general about mental and emotional issues I was having, he apparently didn't realize their severity. His suggestion seemed totally ludicrous to me. I had all I could do to survive my present work in my emotional state, much less add anything else. My response to him was "Unfortunately, I'm in no shape to be concerned with things like that right now." He acted surprised. In a way, I was angry. I had, to some extent, been sparing him of the details of my condition, not wanting to complain or worry him. Now it seemed almost like he was trying to pressure me to move forward in an area of my life that I thought might be more for his ego than mine. After the call, I felt even worse. I had had to admit, to both him and myself, that I really was having significant mental and emotional problems, and that they, in fact, were interfering with my life.

As was often the case, I felt a bit better by bedtime that Sunday evening. After several hours of relaxing and easy reading in the late evenings, I tended to feel my best for the day. That night, I wanted to get to bed a bit early to help ensure that I got enough sleep to be at my best the next day. Besides a busy day at work the next day, there was an evening Sunday School teacher's meeting at church on Monday evening.

I really looked forward to teaching Sunday School again. I have taught for much of my adult life. Early on, as a young adult, I had a fascination with kids and wanted to study their behaviors and philosophy and learn from them. Gradually over time this fascination waned. But I still enjoyed working with the kids, and feeling a sense of connection with the parents. I had last taught Sunday School the week before my brain aneurysm. Shortly after I got out of the hospital, Sunday School had ended for the summer. It would be starting up again early in the fall. The meeting on Monday evening was to assign grade levels and plan the early curriculum. This would be a big step towards getting back to normal for me. It would give me a chance to help others and think about something besides my health that I had been thinking so much about since my brain aneurysm.

I was in bed by about 10PM on Sunday night. My thoughts kept wandering back to that day's conversation with my father. "He has some nerve!", I told myself. Though consciously I was aware that in fact he was likely unaware of the severity of my emotional issues, I still felt annoyed. I felt a bit smug, in fact, as I drifted off to sleep. "Well he may have the best intentions in mind for me, he sure does come up with some stupid ideas. I guess for just about anything he suggests, doing the opposite is probably a good strategy." With the smugness, and being pleasantly relaxed by an evening of easy reading, I drifted off to sleep fairly quickly.

Just as soon as I had fallen asleep, I had my first nightmare about my brain aneurysm. In the dream, I found myself regaining consciousness beside my bed in much the same manner as had happened the night of my aneurysm. I realized in the dream that I had had another stroke, and I needed to call 911 for help. But I couldn't get to the phone. Then, once I got to the phone, it would not work. I woke up sweating, and for a brief period was not sure whether what had happened had been a dream or real. I got up out of bed and walked around the room. "Do I need to call 911?", I asked myself. "Yes, I've just had another stroke." But no, it seems like it wasn't real – it was a dream. Slowly, I went over the situation in my mind. I remembered the evening – how I had read, then went to bed, then been thinking about the conversation with my father. I had not, in fact, woken up from unconsciousness unable to get to the phone. No, that had been a dream. I went over the events in my mind several times. I walked out into the next room and talked to my cat. Yes, it had just been a bad dream.

I returned to bed, shaken. I was totally unable to sleep the rest of the night. I just laid in bed, feeling worse and worse. Then the thought crossed my mind. "Oh crap, I can't afford to stay awake tonight of all nights!

Tomorrow is Monday and I've got a lot to do at work. Plus the Sunday School teacher's meeting! Please God, not tonight!", I prayed. Trying to relax and drift off to sleep did no good. I would toss and turn, get up and use the bathroom, and check the clock. 2AM. 3AM. 4AM. 5AM. I was going to have to address this problem. I needed to see a doctor to get something for sleep. I needed to see a psychologist for help dealing with the anxiety and depression. And there was no way I would be able to work a difficult day at work, make arrangements for a doctor appointment, and then attend the evening Sunday School teacher's meeting. In fact, I realized I was in no shape to teach Sunday School either.

Once it was 6AM, I knew my father would be up. I needed someone to talk to. I called to confide to him. I heard him answer the phone, in a somewhat gruff voice "Hello....". In the background, I heard church music. My father was listening to the Bible Broadcasting Network – his favorite radio station – while doing morning exercises on his exercise bicycle. I explained the nightmare and lack of sleep I had experienced overnight. I told him I didn't think I would be able to work, much less teach. In fact, I confided, I think I have been just ignoring all the problems, hoping they will go away. I needed to address them. I took as little time off as possible from work after my brain aneurysm, and I tried to ignore the mental symptoms. Now I needed to take the time to resolve the issues. We talked for about a half hour. I discussed my plans with him. Then I got up and got to work doing what I needed to do.

First I sent an E-mail to my boss at work. "Out Again With Complications" was the subject. I explained the sleep and emotional issues, which he was vaguely familiar with but did not know the severity of. I explained that I was likely going to be out from work for a while – I wanted to take the time to see the doctors I needed to and to rest. Then I sent an E-mail to the secretary at my church, asking to be added back to the prayer list. I sent a copy to the Sunday School superintendent, and said I would not be able to teach again until further notice. The next thing I needed to do was get an appointment with my doctor. But it was only 7AM. My doctor's office would not be open for another couple of hours. As the sun shone through my window, I felt miserable. With the excitement, it seemed like a holiday. But no, far from that. The tiredness, anxiety, and nausea let me know how bad of shape my body was presently in. To look forward to, I had more doctor's appointments – as if the nearly weekly followups relating to the brain aneurysm itself were not already enough.

The phone rang. It was my father. "You asked if I had any other advice for you?", he said. "Yes." "I do. Listen to BBN (Bible Broadcasting Network). It's very relaxing to me. God is there for you." I replied that I would give it a try. "And are you reading through your Bible?", he asked. In recent years, I had been reading a devotional book which contained meditations on a different Bible verse each day. I replied that I was reading that. "That's not enough!", he said. "Read through the Good Book. I read mine every morning!" I was confident of my faith in

God and my relationship with Jesus. I had read through the Bible several times as a young adult, but in recent years I was "too busy" to do that. Now, I guess I no longer had an excuse not to. I agreed to give BBN a try, and to begin reading through my Bible, at a rate which would allow me to read through the whole Bible in a year (the same rate I had used before when I read through the Bible several times as a young adult).

Replies began coming in to my E-mails. The church secretary affirmed that she had added me back to the prayer list. My boss sent back a reply to the effect of "Whatever you need to do, Frank, we're here for you! Just keep us informed." It was now late enough to call my doctor. I talked to the receptionist. She suggested that she had an appointment available early the following week. "I can't wait that long!", I said "I am not even able to work, the problem is so severe! I didn't sleep more than an hour all night last night!" Seeing the seriousness of the situation, she agreed to get me in that afternoon. I breathed a sigh of relief.

My doctor asked me about my symptoms. "Didn't you have issues with insomnia once before?", he asked? Back in 2001, I had experienced symptoms of anxiety, depression, and insomnia. "Yes, back in 2001, shortly after I moved to Buffalo", I replied. "What did we do about it then?", he asked. I recalled that, for sleep, I had been given klonopin. I also had been given an antidepressant (prozac), which I had been on since. "Well, let's do the klonopin again.", he said. "It worked before, so chances are it will work now as well." "How long will I need to take that?", I asked, recalling that that medication has a reputation for being addictive. "Six months? A year? Two years? I really don't care, I'll prescribe it as long as you need it.", he said. "The brain often takes a year or two to recover from trauma. Now – what about psychological issues – are you getting some counseling?" Way back in 2001, I had started seeing a psychologist for anxiety and depression. Even after these issues resolved, I had continued seeing him a few times a year (at my own expense), because he was acting as sort of a problem-solving "coach" for me. I had seen him most recently about a month earlier, before my symptoms had gotten as severe as they were now. At that time, his next available appointment was not until several months later, and I had not pursued anything earlier since my problems were not as severe at that time. I explained the scheduling to my doctor. "Well, that's unacceptable!", he said. "You need counseling now. I have a list of psychologists here. One of these will be able to get you in right away." The doctor then wrote me a prescription for klonopin. Because klonopin is a controlled substance, he would not be able to call in the prescription to the pharmacy – I would need to take the prescription over there myself and have it filled.

As I left the doctor's office, I had to sign papers saying that I realized that klonopin can be addictive, and that it is a controlled substance. That I would not share my prescription with anyone else. I had been on klonopin several times before in my life, so I thought nothing of signing these. Little did I know that I would soon become addicted.

I picked up the prescription from the pharmacy. I felt relieved to know that I would no doubt be able to sleep that night. I went home and started calling psychologists on the list, to see if any had openings soon. I found one with an opening in two days, at the same office as the psychologist I had been seeing as a coach in recent years. I made the appointment. Over the phone, they took medical history – including information on which other psychologists I had seen in the past.

I checked my Email again – no new messages. I was finally getting things in order, and could relax. It was late afternoon. I called my father and gave him an update on what had transpired. I laid down and rested. I tried listening to BBN, as my father had suggested. But it seemed to be making me worse. The old-time music made me feel like a young child in my father's house again – disconcerting in my emotional state. As I listened to sermons by elderly preachers, I got the feeling of someone who had lived their life and was now preparing for their death. That was the last thing I wanted to think about – I still had life ahead of me, or so I hoped anyway. So I settled into easy reading and relaxing for a while. In the evening I took a walk. I no longer felt so tired. Having made so much progress towards addressing my illness that day, I felt an increased sense of confidence. I felt better than I had in several days. Shortly before bedtime, I took a klonopin tablet. Sure enough, it relaxed me even more. I slept well that night, and even slept in an extra hour or so since I was taking off work for my illness.

Around lunch time the next day, I got a call from the psychologist I had been seeing as a coach in recent years. He asked me why I was going to see another psychologist (they both worked at the same office). I explained that he had had no appointments available in the near future, and that my doctor had wanted me to see someone sooner. He explained that he did not have any regular appointments available, but that since the situation was now urgent, he could get me in if needed. Thinking this through, though, I still liked the idea of seeing a new psychologist. I saw my previous psychologist more as a coach presently. I had been talking to him for many years. It might be good to get fresh insights from someone new. I explained that I wanted to keep him as a coach, but would go ahead and try someone new to address the specific problems I was now facing. He agreed to that.

I was scheduled to see the new psychologist the following morning. I was very much looking forward to seeing someone new for a new sense of perspective. But when I got into his office, he seemed upset about something. "I see that you have been seeing someone else here – are you going to stop seeing him?", he asked. "No", I explained, "I will continue to see him as a coach. But I want to see you about my present issues of anxiety and insomnia". "Well that is not ethical by any means, and I refuse to see you in that case." He explained that two psychologists may have differing philosophies, and that it was not medically ethical for two people to treat the same patient. Now being forced to choose between him and my previous psychologist, I decided to stick with the old one who I knew well. The initial consultation with the new psychologist that I had looked forward to, and was scheduled to last 50 minutes, was over in less than 10 minutes. I called my old psychologist and set up some appointments. Fortunately, he was able to get me in several times over the next couple weeks. But I felt disappointed that I was no longer going to get insights from someone new. And now, I wouldn't get any new insights to make progress on my illness for several more days.

LOUD TEENS

I took the rest of the week off work sick. Since I had already used all my sick time for my hospitalization, I used vacation time for this. That would mean no chance to take any vacation that year, but I didn't feel up to going on a vacation anyway. I hoped to get more rest during the week to make up for my recent lack of sleep. As such, I tried napping during the day. But I found I could not sleep. It was only later that I learned that napping during the day is one of the worst things you can do for insomnia. But I was now taking klonopin for sleep, so at at least in the short term, I was sleeping okay at night.

During the week, I had two appointments with my psychologist. I looked forward to these appointments, hoping in some sense that he would have major insights and "magic" solutions to the psychological problems I was facing. Yet after each appointment, I left disappointed. I had a bunch of notes about things I wanted to cover with him. Yet it seemed in each 50-minute appointment I barely had time to scratch the surface in terms of things I wanted to go over. His main advice, from a psychological perspective, was to practice what he called "Mindfulness Meditation"[5]. In this meditation, one concentrates on the sensations of their breath and tries to dismiss any other thoughts that arise during the meditation. I was somewhat familiar with relaxation techniques already. Since high school, I had practiced at times a technique similar to Herbert Benson's Relaxation Response[6]. In the past, I had found this technique helpful. However, I also knew from past experiences with anxiety issues that I was unable to successfully practice this technique when the anxiety I was experiencing was too severe. It was pure torture to sit still that long, and I felt far worse afterwards for the effort. I did give Mindfulness Meditation a try during walks however. I would take a few minutes to concentrate on my breath and try to dismiss any other thoughts that arose during my efforts. While I was able to do this, I did not find it helpful.

Would it help me to get out into nature to relax? I didn't think so, but thought it might be worth a try. In the past, one of my favorite natural sights was Niagara Falls, which is only about an hour from where I live. I thought of going there. However, this would require going into Canada. I had not been to Canada in several years. While I did have a passport, I was concerned that I may run into issues crossing the border back into the US, as had happened once before. In my sensitized state, I wasn't

---

[5]   See book by Kabat-Zinn, Jon in Bibliography.
[6]   See book by Benson, Herbert in Bibliography.

sure I wanted to risk this issue possibly arising, even though it was probably not very likely.

When I mentioned the possibility of visiting Niagara Falls to my psychologist, he got a concerned look on his face. I asked him what bothered him about me going to Niagara Falls. Though at first, he just said he thought crossing the border would be stressful, his look belied bigger concerns, so I pressed him on this issue. Finally he asked "You're not planning to commit suicide by going over Niagara Falls, are you?" That comment came as a surprise to me. Despite the intensity of my suffering, I never seriously considered suicide. Based on my studies of religion, near-death experiences, and altered states of consciousness, I had long ago become convinced that we are put on Earth for a purpose. Life is a school, and we need to grow and learn our curriculum. At times, I did have a passing concern that I might do something desperate on the spur of the moment – jump in front of a car, for example while out walking – but this was an idle concern and more of an anxiety issue than an actual significant possibility.

Anyway, my psychologist recommended, since I liked Niagara Falls but was concerned about crossing the border into Canada, that I instead visit Letchworth State Park, an hour or two drive away. That park, what I had never previously visited, had streams and small waterfalls and was less crowded by far than Niagara Falls. Perhaps it would be a relaxing place to go. So later that week, since I was already taking vacation time from work for my illness anyway, I decided to drive there. But I found the experience to be unpleasant. By myself, with all sorts of families and groups around, I felt lonely. Because the klonopin which I was taking for sleep at night continued to have an effect during the day, I felt slow and had feelings of unreality as I saw the bright natural sights. Then I saw group after group of young campers, and felt the loss at being potentially too old now for outdoor life. Then too, as I did a bit of hiking, I was afraid of getting lost or falling and getting injured. My mind was focused constantly on everything that could go wrong, thus causing even more anxiety. So I took a few pictures, had lunch, and headed for home. Though I was glad I had "accomplished" the trip, it made me feel no better – in fact, I would say it made me feel a little worse.

On Friday (August 23), I requested a conference call with my boss in order to give him an update on my situation and plans for work. While commuting through the construction and detours in Buffalo was stressful, as was hearing all the negative conversations from co-workers around me, staying home was no panacea either. At home, I had little to think about besides my illness. I had long since lost interest in previous hobbies, which now seemed unbearable to do. So I thought that, despite the stress, working was probably the lesser of two evils. When I talked to my boss, I mentioned the issues I was having with all the noise and negative conversations going on around me at work. He told me that he could arrange to have my desk moved to someplace quieter. And, it would be fine with him if I worked from home until arrangements for the move were completed. That would save me the frustrating commute, as well as giving me an extra hour (time normally spent commuting) for relaxing. So the following week I began working from home again, much like I had when I first got out of the hospital. It was a lonely task, but I did get to interact with others through E-mails and the occasional conference call.

While the klonopin was helping with sleep, and helping somewhat with anxiety, it was drastically worsening my depression. I have suffered throughout my life, since at least age 6, from intermittent but rather severe depressions. When I was treated for depression for the fourth time back in 2001, my doctor recommended that I continue taking fluoxetine (Prozac) for the rest of my life. Sure enough, I experienced no episodes of depression from late 2001 up until the time of my brain aneurysm. But a problem with antidepressants is that they can sometimes stop working after a period of time. That appeared to be what was happening. And benzodiazepine drugs, such as klonopin, can worsen depression symptoms. On Friday the 30th of August, I felt particularly depressed all day. My work, while normally (since my brain aneurysm) providing no sense of satisfaction or accomplishment, now became absolute drudgery to do. As I tried to work, my mind would wander to my symptoms, and I would worry about whether I would ever get better. I felt so bad that I began crying during the afternoon as I worked from home. I really needed someone to talk to, but I had no one. I thought of calling my father. But he was having his own problems with arthritis, and besides I didn't want to lean on him given his old age and the fact that he would no longer be around to rely on relatively soon. Fortunately, I got a call that evening from a nurse associated with my insurance company. Apparently, the company calls those who have recently experienced serious medical events to check up on things. The half hour or so I spent talking to her, where I described my experiences, symptoms, and what I had tried in order to get better, was pretty much the only time that day I had felt fairly close to normal. Though I could not distract myself with work or hobbies, talking to someone who might have ideas for a solution to problems related to my illness was engaging enough to briefly hold my attention and keep it off myself. I experienced significant depression on other days as well, but that had been the worst day.

Since I wouldn't be teaching Sunday School, I decided to instead participate in my church's Christian Care and Support program. This is a service where volunteers visit those who have recently experienced significant issues in their lives. I recalled how valuable I had found a bit of assistance with practical matters (getting home from the hospital, getting groceries when I was unable to drive) to be to me, and I thought this was something I might want to do to help others. There was quite a bit of training involved – several large books to read and a training session one evening a week for several months. But the training session would be a lot easier to deal with than teaching Sunday School, would give me social involvement, and the reading would help me learn how to better handle traumatic events myself, plus keep my mind occupied. So I began studying the materials for this course on weekends, and attending the training sessions on Monday evenings. Working from home, I didn't want to become isolated socially. Despite having no desire to do so and it feeling like a Herculean effort to do so, I attended a meeting with the local ham club (where I had was a long-time member). Though a big effort and it did not provide a huge lift, talking to others about topics besides my illness did make me feel a little better.

On Friday the 13th of September, I was still working from home. Late that afternoon, I heard a bit of commotion from the apartment below mine, and realized that someone new was moving in. I had lived in the same apartment for the past 11years. During that time, I had two different downstairs neighbors. The first was very quiet. The second, who had lived in the apartment for the past five years, could sometimes be noisy on weekends during sporting events, but in general were quiet (particularly at night). I remembered I had seen them move out at the end of July. Having someone new move in now was a big concern. In my sensitized state, noise would be very difficult for me to tolerate. I wanted to know more about the people who were moving in, so I watched out my window. I saw a middle-aged woman carrying stuff into the apartment. "Good", I thought to myself. "That is unlikely to be someone who makes a lot of noise." But unfortunately, I then saw two much younger people, who appeared to be teenagers, carrying stuff in. "Maybe they are the movers", I re-assured myself. But as I continued to watch, I realized from their interactions with the woman that they were likely her children. "Crap!", I thought. "That is exactly what I need in my anxious state. Two teenagers to make noise!" Still, though, I didn't want to prejudge them. Yes, they were teens, but maybe they were quiet and well-behaved.

I practically held my breath over the coming hours, just waiting for the loud stereos to start. But I never heard anything, beyond the noise of someone moving furniture around. Perhaps they really were decent people after all. Then on Sunday, as I got home from church, I noticed a cat sitting in my new neighbor's patio window. "Well, anyone who owns a cat can't be all bad.", I told myself. Things had been quiet the past two days and nights. Maybe I had worried for nothing.

As it turned out, my worries had in fact been well-founded. While there was almost no noise the first couple weeks, gradually things changed. Their bathroom is located right below mine. The first noise I heard was the sound of loud music coming from the bathroom as one of my neighbors took a shower. This became more and more frequent, and soon the music would play whenever any of the three of them took a shower – and these showers would often last for 45 minutes or more. As the klonopin I was taking for sleep began to lose its effectiveness, I found myself often awake in the middle of the night. It would be say 1AM in the morning, and I would hear the sounds of screaming and screeching teenagers in the bedroom below me. Then I began to hear loud arguments from the living room below mine during the evenings when I was trying to read. Soon after that, doors began slamming loudly (enough to shake the building) every time someone went in and out of the apartment. A situation like this is certainly not what I needed as I suffered from PTSD from my brain hemorrhage. Even in my younger years, noise had always bothered me a lot more than it bothers most people. Now that I was an "old man", would people just assume I was some old grouch who did not need to be taken seriously when I complained? I wrote a letter of complaint to the apartment managers. So did several other neighbors. Each time, the noise would abate for a short time but come back in a few weeks. Ultimately, these neighbors continued to be a source of stress until the apartment landlord refused to renew their one-year lease when it expired at the end of September, 2014.

MASH, MAC, AND DENT

It seems like many locations associated with medical treatment, at least in the Buffalo area, have names that remind one of violence. My initial diagnosis on the night of my stroke took place at the MAC center. MAC stands for Mercy Ambulatory Care. It is part of the Mercy Hospital system in Buffalo. The name reminded me of either a great big truck that I might be unfortunate enough to get behind while driving, or of a thug with the name "Mac". As I started driving again, I kept getting behind vans that were labeled MASH. MASH is an urgent care center, apparently with headquarters in the Buffalo area. It is pretty amazing how you start noticing things in the world that align with your present fears. I had never noticed either of these prior to my brain hemorrhage, but now each of them served as a painful reminder of illness and injury.

But the worst of all was DENT Neurologic Institute. This name, which I always see written in all capital letters, looks like an acronym. But apparently it is actually the name of one of its founders. From the time I was released from the hospital in May through the end of 2013, I had doctors appointments an average of once a week or more. These appointments were with a variety of doctors. My primary care physician was seeing me to monitor thyroid levels, cholesterol levels with the atorvastatin treatment changes, and the klonopin prescription. My surgeon was seeing me every couple months, as was my neurologist, to monitor my progress and check for neurological deficits. Typically I would also need to go and have a CT scan or MRI scan of the brain done prior to these visits. And of course, I had the psychologist visits as well.

DENT, where my neurologist had his office, was my least favorite place to go. It was certainly more convenient than driving the over 40 miles round trip to see my surgeon. But at DENT, it seems I never failed to see others who reminded me just how bad things could be with neurological problems. There was the lady in her 50s who had had a stroke, and now had severe difficulty both walking and talking. Apparently she had some remaining issues, and wasn't sure how long she would survive. She seemed content with her situation though, saying something like "Well, if I die, I die. If God wants to call me home, I'm ready." Despite her difficulties, she socialized with others just like anyone else would. I had difficulty with socializing given the mental issues caused by PTSD (and I later found out, exacerbated even during the daytime by the klonopin I was taking at night for sleep). There were the drooling teenagers, brought into the office in wheelchairs by their mothers, who constantly made groaning sounds. I never failed to see myself in them, and how I came very close to having that kind of brain damage. I felt sorry for their caregivers. It seemed that the more discouraging the waiting room scene was, the later my doctor would be. It was not unusual to sit there for well over an hour.

By mid-September, my boss was asking when I would be coming into work in person again (I continued to work from home). He offered to move my desk and computer so I didn't have to sit so close to the distracting and depressing conversations. He took snapshots of several places around the work area with his phone and sent them to me, asking which I would prefer. Since there were no walls or cubicles in the office area when I worked, there was no real good spot. I settled on a spot a few feet away from a project manager. I knew that this project manager spends a lot of time on the phone, and that this would be a distraction. However, I also knew that this manager talked about nothing besides work. No political arguments or "state of the world" discussions. While distracting, this conversation would not be depressing. I felt I could deal with someone discussing technical aspects of projects with clients over the phone. And I was glad to be able to get back to work and at least have some minimal amount of social interaction. I let my boss know my choice, and a few days later he E-mailed me saying that the move was complete.

On Wednesday September 18th, I went into work for the first time in over a month. I had hoped getting back around people would help me forget my illness, but it actually made things worse initially. I felt almost a phobic reaction to seeing the familiar sights at work again. It felt like I had "failed" coming back to work the first time, and now I was making another pitiful effort to return a second time. The lights above where my desk was now located did not work, so the atmosphere seemed gloomy. An air conditioning vent continuously blew cold air at me, and though the inside temperature was not particularly cold, I found myself constantly shivering. At lunch, when I had hoped for a relaxing walk, I was constantly walking by jack hammers and detouring for closed sidewalks due to the continued intensive construction downtown Buffalo. I looked for other places to walk, but everyplace nearby was either torn up or in a neighborhood of questionable safety. And with my commute to and from work and the now shorter daylight hours, I was now getting home too late to take an evening walk before dark.

Even with all the above issues, though, I was, in a way, glad to be back at work again. I could at least maintain some hope that I was getting back to normal again. I was able to do my work, attend meetings, and even do a small amount of socializing from time to time. I had the lights above my desk repaired so that my work area was no longer as gloomy, and the air conditioning vent directed in another direction away from my desk.

There was one more negative surprise waiting for me at work. With the rapid expansion of the medical infrastructure downtown Buffalo, part of the building I worked in was now being rented out to medical therapists. In the break room, I saw a sign advertising something about "neurological injury therapy" and a list of types of injury covered. "Traumatic head injury. Stroke. Multiple Sclerosis". One morning when I attempted to use the restroom, I found a walker blocking the door. Inside was a young man being assisted by another man in getting to the toilet. I stood nearby and waited a good ten minutes for the restroom to be free. It is the only restroom on that floor. The same situation continued to recur. Sometimes I would be in the middle of a conference call and need to walk away briefly to use the restroom. Instead of being gone for a minute or two from the call, I would be gone ten minutes or more while I waited for a neurologically impaired person and his assistant to complete their restroom trip. Sometimes the toilet was in use or blocked by the two people moving slowly across the room. Other times the sink was blocked. Besides the obvious inconvenience of the delay in using the restroom, particularly when I needed to get back to a meeting or conference call, seeing the neurologically damaged person once again served as a painful reminder of my stroke and the impairment I was presently suffering from. In the restroom, I would hear a droning sound as the brain-damaged person said incomprehensible things like "Oh! Undulator! Undulator!", and his assistant agreed "Yeah, undulator...." While having to deal with things like this may seem trivial to a "normal" person, in my highly sensitized state is was pure torture.

Other issues, which would under normal circumstances be simply an annoyance, also got thrown in, and they would seem like huge problems and add to my anxiety. For example, in October my primary care physician changed the dose of my thyroid medicine. The dose has changed occasionally, up or down, since I was first diagnosed hypothyroid back in 1990. No big deal. But insurance this time was the issue. In order to be eligible for any prescription drug coverage, the insurance company my employer had recently changed to required all long-term prescriptions to be filled through the mail-order pharmacy they were affiliated with. That meant allowing extra time for delivery, so I had to be sure to refill prescriptions at least a week before I ran out. The problem was that my doctor's office and the new mail order pharmacy I was now required to use did not communicate. Each month, I would check online to see if my prescription had been filled, and would find no record of it. I would call my doctor's office, and be told that they had electronically transmitted the prescription to the mail-order pharmacy already, but that they would go ahead and send it again. I would then call the pharmacy, and they would tell me that the prescription would not show up in their system for as long as 3 days, and that I should call back then. Three days later, I would call and they would say they had no record of the prescription order being received, and that I should contact my doctor. My doctor's office would say that they had sent the prescription twice now, and that I needed to contact the pharmacy. One month I literally spent several hours going back an forth on the phone between the two parties, all the while images of running out of vital medicines raced through my mind.

Each evening when I got home from work, I would have dinner. One good thing was that my appetite was improving. Though I still had a feeling of slight nausea and butterflies in my stomach much of the time, I now no longer had trouble consuming a reasonable amount of calories each day. My weight stabilized and was no longer dropping. Since darkness prevented an evening walk, I did light exercises for a brief period each evening. After dinner, I always tried my best to relax. I found that the most relaxing and reassuring thing I could do was to read. I would read my old diary entries from past episodes of anxiety and depression and re-assure myself that I had overcame such issues in the past. I would read inspirational books by such authors as Norman Vincent Peale, who I had found quite helpful previously. Sometimes I would watch a bit of TV, though I have never as an adult been much of a TV fan. I would spend time petting and playing with my pet cat. I went to bed around 10PM each night. I would take klonopin about an hour before that. The hour between when I took the klonopin and when I went to bed was often the most peaceful and the time when I felt least anxious and depressed. I allowed myself 8 ½ hours to sleep, getting up at 6:30. Even with the klonopin, I sometimes laid awake for a couple of hours later in the night. But I was now getting a sufficient amount of sleep most nights.

Since I was not teaching Sunday School, I wanted to find something else I could do for my church. In order to be of some service and to get more social interaction. My church had been very helpful to me by providing transportation home from the hospital, and to get groceries when I had been unable to drive. I asked what program had provided these services, and was told that this ministry is called Christian Caregiving. Becoming a Christian Caregiver required quite a bit of training – twelve evenings of two-hour classes, plus much reading of material between classes. I expressed an interest, and was given the reading material. After looking through the material, I decided this might be a good way for me to serve. I certainly had the time to read the material each week. The classes were held on Monday evenings and concluded by 9PM, so they would not interfere with my sleep. So I committed to taking the course. Each weekend I spent several hours reading the training material, and I attended the classes on Monday evenings. After a long day of work in my sensitized state, I would generally feel pretty frazzled on Monday evenings, and not having time to relax in the evening sometimes made it take longer than usual to fall asleep at night. But I did get a small sense of accomplishment from learning the material, as well a chance for social interaction. So, at least at some level, I did look forward to the training each Monday evening.

During the month of October, I was basically "holding my own". Things were no longer going rapidly downhill like they had been in the summer. My weight has stabilized, and I had a reasonable appetite. Taking the klonopin, I was able to get a sufficient amount of sleep. At work, I was able to accomplish the tasks I needed to, and do a small amount of socializing. Though not usually

ADDICTED TO KLONOPIN

I was first diagnosed with anxiety and clinical depression late in 1990, following thyroid issues. For all my life, I had suffered occasionally from severe anxiety. In college, I always thought there was something wrong with my thyroid, based on the symptoms I experienced, but a thyroid test had indicated that my values were in the normal range. In 1990, I had strong hypothyroid symptoms once again. I had difficulty concentrating, very dry skin, constipation, and an oral temperature of 97.4, more than 1 degree below the normal 98.6. With severe difficulty concentrating beginning to interfere with my ability to work in late 1990, I had a series of medical tests. It was found that I was severely hypothyroid. I was started on thyroid replacement medication. Within days of starting the thyroid supplement, I began experiencing severe anxiety (to the point where I couldn't even concentrate well enough to read a book), heart palpitations, insomnia, and depression. I kept going back to the internist who had diagnosed my thyroid condition, saying something else was wrong. After she was unable to find anything despite numerous medical tests, she said she felt the issue was psychological, and recommended that I see a psychiatrist. The psychiatrist diagnosed me with major anxiety and clinical depression, a likely result of having had low thyroid levels over an extended period of time. He recommended that I take two drugs – an antidepressant (prozac), and a sedative (klonopin). Even at that time in my life, I was very hesitant to take medicines that affected my mind, after having vague recollections of horror stories from people getting addicted to them. However, my symptoms were so bad that I could not sleep, work, or even read. I was a "walking dead" person. So reluctantly I agreed. Although symptoms became even worse initially when I began taking the medicines, within several weeks there was a dramatic improvement. Within six weeks, my anxiety and depression were completely gone, and I was back to my "old self". The psychiatrist at that point tapered me off the klonopin, and several months later discontinued the prozac.

I continued to suffer bouts of anxiety and depression at various times after that. The majority of the time I had no symptoms, but occasionally, particularly when I was experiencing a lot of stress in my life, major anxiety and depression would occur. Although I tried several different medicines prescribed by various psychiatrists and doctors, we always found that the combination of Prozac and klonopin was what I ultimately needed to get rid of my anxiety and depression. In 2001, I was going through my fourth diagnosed incidence of major anxiety and depression. Although I tapered off the klonopin as soon as I was doing better, my psychiatrist recommended that I stay on the Prozac "for life", due to my past history of recurring anxiety and depression (this was the fourth time I had been diagnosed). Therefore, from 2001 on, I had been taking 20mg of Prozac daily. And during the nearly 12 years from late 2001 through the time of my brain hemorrhage, I didn't experience any significant anxiety or depression.

When I went to my primary care physician with my anxiety and insomnia problems in August, he said he recalled that I had been treated for anxiety and depression before. He asked me what worked for me in the past. I replied "klonopin and prozac". Since I was already on Prozac for the past 12 years, my doctor recommended that I add klonopin. It seemed like a logical step to me at the time, so I agreed. However, what I wasn't fully aware of was that previously, we had used klonopin just as a temporary measure to help with the additional anxiety experienced when starting Prozac. And it was for a very limited time, with tapering beginning after less than two months. Now though, my doctor was prescribing that I take klonopin over an extended period of time. I asked him "How long do you think I will need to take this?" He replied "A few months – maybe a couple years – it's hard to say. It can take the brain that long to stabilize after trauma. I have no problem prescribing it for as long as you need it."

I should have been wary at this point. I was told that, because klonopin is a benzodiazepine, it is a controlled substance. Recent law changes meant that I would have to hand-carry my prescription to the pharmacist – it could not be sent electronically. Further, because of it being a controlled substance, no refills were allowed on the prescription. I would have to get a new prescription from my doctor when that one ran out. "When you need a new prescription, just call and I will write you one.", he said. I also had to sign a paper saying that I was aware that klonopin was a controlled substance and had the potential for addiction "if misused". At the pharmacy, I picked up my prescription for 60 0.5mg tablets of klonopin. The instructions said "Take one tablet, twice daily as needed". So, on August 19th, I began taking one klonopin tablet every night at bedtime, as I had done several times previously when starting on Prozac.

The klonopin worked well initially. I was finally getting some sleep again. Yet it began to lose its effectiveness within a few weeks. For example, on September 3rd I needed to get up at 5AM for a work implementation. Due to anticipatory anxiety, I found myself awake and unable to go back to sleep shortly after 3AM, despite having taken klonopin at bedtime. On the night of September 11th, I was woke up by storms in the middle of the night, and it took a couple of hours to get back to sleep. Most nights in September and October I was sleeping about 6 out of 8 hours. Not great – but since it was certainly better than it had been in August, I assumed I should continue taking the klonopin. I now know from research that benzodiazepines such as klonopin are only effective for sleep for a few weeks at most if taken each night.

In addition, the klonopin was definitely making my depression worse. Whereas I had experienced mostly anxiety prior to starting klonopin, I began experiencing moderate depression within a week or two after starting the klonopin. The depression was particularly severe during September.

The first hint of addiction to klonopin came in October, although I didn't realize the cause at the time. In late September, I had my thyroid levels tested for the first time since my brain surgery. The tests indicated that my thryoid levels were slightly low, so my doctor prescribed a slightly higher dose of thyroid replacement medication. Thyroid levels do vary with time, so occasional adjustments (up or down) are required. I had needed to make adjustments several times in the past. I never experienced significant issues from these minor adjustments. The new prescribed dose was a slight increase, but still well within the range of my past dosage experience. Within a few days after I started taking the increased dosage of thyroid medication, I began to experience anxiety and akathisia during the late afternoon and early evening hours. I attributed this to the increase in thyroid supplement dosage. While I didn't normally experience issues with changing the dosage of thyroid medication, I reasoned that I was in a sensitized state this time, and thus experiencing symptoms. In retrospect, I believe that what was happening is that the increased thyroid hormone dose slightly speeded up my metabolism. This resulted in faster breakdown of the klonopin I was taking at bedtime, leading to withdrawal symptoms beginning in the late afternoon.

Throughout October, I continued to experience the akathisia, beginning in the middle of each afternoon, and continuing into early evening. I was puzzled. Could I still be experiencing symptoms from increasing the thyroid hormone after this long? Was I somehow developing new symptoms as part of my anxiety? I got my answer one day in early November. The night before, I had slept very poorly. Of particular note was that it took me hours to get to sleep. While I often experienced difficulty sleeping later in the night, that night had been unusual in that I had difficulty falling asleep initially. I had actually slept pretty well later in the night. That day though, I experienced severe anxiety and akathisia not just during the late afternoon and early evening, but throughout the entire day. And it was far worse than usual. I remember sitting in a meeting, trying to concentrate, but feeling anxious, spacey, and like I was acting in a dream. "What is going on here?", I kept asking myself. I felt so much worse than usual. While stress certainly exacerbated my symptoms in general, this day was not particularly stressful. So what was different about that day? And what was different about the night before where I had experienced unusual difficulty getting to sleep? Did I eat something different? Do something different? Then it dawned on me. Maybe I had somehow forgotten to take the klonopin the night before? I had a list that I checked off each night when I took my medicines and vitamins. I had checked it off the night before. But maybe I had missed that particular medicine? When I got home from work, I counted the number of tablets I had remaining in the klonopin bottle. I knew how many tablets had been prescribed to date, that I took one tablet every night, and the number of days I had been taking it. Sure enough, I found that I had one extra tablet. So either the pharmacist had included one extra tablet, or else I had missed the previous night. I suspected the later. And sure enough, when I took the klonopin late that evening, I suddenly felt much better.

I did research online for my late afternoon symptoms. Sure enough, the most common matches I found were "benzodiazepine withdrawal". I began to learn of the horrors of benzodiazepine addiction through a number of forums that were devoted entirely to supporting people who are discontinuing benzodiazepines. I learned that the majority of people who found themselves addicted to benzos were not drug abusers, but were people who had taken these medicines exactly as they had been prescribed by their doctors. There was talk online that these drugs were more difficult to get off of than heroin! What a scary thought! It seemed really hard to believe that a drug prescribed by a doctor could be this bad. Unconvinced, I found an online forum devoted to recreational drug usage. Besides their medical uses, benzos could also be used to "get high". And of course, people who used them in this way often found themselves addicted. I found instances of people who had been addicted (at different times) to both heroin and to benzos. Sure enough, some said that they had a more difficult time kicking benzos than they had kicking heroin! Not all agreed, but the two were clearly comparable in difficulty to get off of.

I continued to do more research on benzodiazepines each evening. I soon found plenty of medical studies that indicated numerous long-term negative effects of continued benzodiazepine use[789]. I learned that discontinuing benzodiazepines is something that has to be done very gradually, over a period of months or even years (depending on the dosage and how long someone has been taking them). Even with such a slow discontinuation, symptoms could be debilitating, and they are usually not completely over even once the final tablet is taken.

After many evenings or research, I knew I needed to get off of the klonopin. Per my research (which included not only forums but also medical publications), I learned that it had no positive effects on sleep beyond a couple weeks. I had been on it for nearly three months. I made a tentative discontinuation schedule. I would cut back by

---

[7] The effects of benzodiazepines on cognition, <u>J Clin Psychiatry.</u> 2005;66 Suppl 2:9-13, <u>http://www.ncbi.nlm.nih.gov/ pubmed/15762814</u>.

[8] Brain Damage from Benzodiazepines: The Troubling Facts, Risks, and History of Minor Tranquilizers, <u>Psychology Today</u>, November 18, 2010, http://www.psychologytoday.com/blog/ side-effects/201011/brain-damage-benzodiazepines-the-troubling-facts-risks-and-history-minor-tr.

[9] See book by Hobson-Dupont, Jack and Mercer, Robert E. in Bibliography.

25%, once a month. This would allow me to be entirely free of the drug in four months. This was considered a fast taper, with a 10 to 20 percent reduction each month being a more typical rate. I reasoned, however, that I had only been on the klonopin for about 3 months. Many people had been on it for years. Also, my dosage of 0.5mg per day was a small one. Many people who found themselves addicted to klonopin had been prescribed increasing doses by their doctor as its effectiveness diminished, and were thus taking 1 or 2mg a day or even more. I joined the BenzoBuddies forum[10] for support.

On Friday November 15th, I did my first klonopin cut. I broke a tablet in half, then broke one of the half tablets in half, and took one half plus one quarter of the tablet for a total of 75% (25 percent reduction). And surprisingly, I slept fairly well that night. That was to become a pattern. I found that each time I cut the dosage, I tended to still sleep fairly well the first night. Sleep problems would generally begin a few days after the cut, and last a week or so before sleep returned to its previous quality. The afternoon akathisia would worsen slightly during the same period. On a positive note, it seemed that each time I made a cut in dosage, I would feel significantly less depressed for a day or two. A couple of times on the day after a cut, I felt almost like my normal self. This improvement did not last, but experiencing it was reassuring.

---

[10] http://www.benzobuddies.org.

During the time that I was tapering off the klonopin, I spent an average of two hours each evening on the BenzoBuddies forum. This forum was helpful to me for several reasons. First of all, there were many people on the forum who were far worse off than I was. Many of them were completely incapable of working during their withdrawal; some had lost their houses or their spouses during the ordeal. Although my symptoms continued to be extremely uncomfortable, I realized how much better off I was then them because I was still able to work and take care of things in my life. Second, there were plenty of success stories – people who had gone through far worse benzo withdrawal than I was going through and eventually recovered completely and were back to living a full life. These stories provided me with encouragement. Third, I found that the forums provided a good distraction for keeping my mind off of my situation. Since my brain aneurysm, I had focused almost entirely on survival. When I tried to get interested in other hobbies I had previously enjoyed, I found the experience empty and it made me feel worse. Presumably because this was about getting better, I felt motivated when I was in the forums. And I also enjoyed being able to help other people. I had done plenty of my own research on benzodiazepines. Many people in the forum had questions I could answer. And I even got a chance to use some of my "engineering skills" from time to time. Often someone would ask a question like "I cut my dosage of X benzodiazepine by 20% last Thursday. So how much less of it is in my body today?" I would then look up the half-life of the benzodiazepine in question, calculate the remaining amount based on the two dosages and time that had passed, and post the answer. Not everyone was able to do such calculations themselves, so it made me feel useful. I also noticed that I was developing more compassion for people. A number of people in the forum had become addicted to benzodiazepines during treatment for alcoholism. Given the fact that I am a non-drinker, and had many bad experiences with dorm mates who abused alcohol during college, I had always felt a disdain and lack of compassion for anyone whose alcohol use had caused them problems. But now I found myself being more compassionate. Someone who had been an alcoholic and then became addicted to benzodiazepines prescribed for treatment would post how he thought his life was ruined. I was able to re-assure them with statistics about benzodiazapine recovery.

I continued cutting the klonopin dosage by 25% each month. Finally, on February 14th, I made my final cut – to no klonopin. As with the other cuts, I experienced some problems with insomnia and akathisia shortly after the cut. Within two months, however, I recovered from the withdrawal symptoms completely. From mid-April through much of the summer, I had only two or three nights where sleeping was a problem – pretty much back to normal. Akathisia was also mostly absent during this period. I still continued to experience some degree of anxiety and depression, but that had been the case even before I had started on the klonopin.

CHRISTMAS PAST

As a very young child, Christmas was always my favorite time of year. I remember liking Christmas so much that I would play Christmas songs on my record player throughout the entire year to remind me of Christmas. But as I got older, that changed. I remember even in late childhood often being disappointed when Christmas finally arrived. Things I received for Christmas never lived up to my expectations. With me and my parents both home for extended periods during the holiday, often we would get on each others nerves and end up arguing about things.

When I graduated from college and began working, I had more reasons to dislike Christmas. Now I no longer had much time off, unlike the extended vacations I got at Christmas during my school years. I remember my first Christmas after getting out of college I only got one day off, and did not have any vacation time left to take additional time. Besides that, where I lived at the time required me to drive past the town's shopping mall in order to get home from work each night. I remember the frustration of sitting through numerous stoplight cycles each evening because so many people were going in and out of the mall. Then too, I enjoyed snow and always looked forward to winter. But often in the weeks before Christmas in Virginia where I lived temperatures would be in the 60s with no snow in sight. Any snow in Virginia usually came later in the winter. That annoyed me as well. In later years, I did manage to take more time off for Christmas, and I lived where snow for Christmas, or at least the first snow by Christmas, was common. Still, I was never a big fan of the season. Too commercial for me. Still too many hassles if I needed to go into the crowds in a store to buy some household item. Too many people at work away or getting sick because of lack of sleep during the Christmas season. Each year, my favorite part of the Christmas season was when it was over and things could start getting back to normal on January 2nd.

I was dreading the approach of the Christmas season in 2013. I knew Christmas is normally a low time for me. This year I was dealing with numerous after-effects of my ruptured brain aneurysm as well, and in the middle of a difficult withdrawal from the klonopin, which I had become addicted to. I was still just barely surviving – getting my work done, at least mostly, at work, then spending the evenings participating in klonopin withdrawal support groups and trying to relax.

Where I live in downtown Orchard Park, there are speakers that play music throughout the year. During

December, this becomes Christmas music. On weekends, I would walk to get some exercise and help get my mind off my situation. Hearing the familiar Christmas music from my childhood and earlier adult days only served to depress me more. Hearing a song I had enjoyed as a child, I would have a vague recollection of some past Christmas. But, since I was suffering from depression, this would be mixed with a vague sense of "something wrong", some negative event from a specific Christmas that I couldn't quite recall. Then, with no vacation time available at work due to having used all my vacation time for sick leave, it reminded me of some of my earlier days as a young adult when I was frustrated with the Christmas season. The memory of younger adulthood would then itself trigger feelings of loss about how long ago that was, and that I was now an "old man". So it was a very negative situation – Christmas songs and other Christmas sites triggering memories of vaguely unpleasant times, which themselves were now gone. I questioned if I would ever be recovered enough to experience even the mixed emotions of past Christmases, let alone any positive times (which were very difficult to recall in my depressed state).

Work was little better. Most days, it was a matter of "survival" - getting through the work day, as my concentration and problem-solving abilities were severely strained in the mental state I was in. On rare days, things would go somewhat better – always for a brief period though. For example, I recall that one day the work problems I faced were relatively benign, and I was making good progress on them. As lunchtime approached, I got an E-mail announcement of a special lunch being offered in celebration of the season. I had forgotten about that event previously, not paying much attention to the original announcement given my poor appetite. But on this day, my appetite was better, and I actually felt felt a brief sense of positive anticipation for the lunch that would occur shortly. Unfortunately, the event would also feature something else – Christmas music. Once I started hearing Christmas songs, my mood once again sank. I tried to stay near the music as short of a time as possible – just long enough to pick up the food and then go back to my desk. It was almost like a phobia – I needed to get out of that area as soon as possible. As well, for the rest of the day, others now in the "Christmas spirit" conversed loudly with each other, distracting me from my work and making me feel isolated.

Knowing that Christmas is often a "down" season for me, I reasoned that if I could get through that, things would be improving from there. That gave me something positive to concentrate on. Also, I was making progress with the klonopin withdrawal. By Christmas day, I was down to half of my original dose. Christmas came and went. I had made it through the Christmas season, and despite all the negatives, was actually feeling slightly better than I had earlier in the fall. This was an encouraging sign. Then came New Years Day, and with that, the long holiday season was now over, and things would be looking up.

Feeling slightly better with the holiday season now behind, I wondered if I could take any small steps towards doing things I enjoyed in my life. In the summer, I had looked forward to teaching Sunday School again. That dream was shattered with the events of August. During the fall, I had attended adult Sunday School – something I very rarely did since previously I was always teaching kids during Sunday School time. I was not enjoying adult Sunday School at all. The material we were covering, a series called "Go Fish", seemed designed to engender a guilt trip if one was not constantly evangelizing to their friends. I never had been one to try to force my views on others, and I was presently having enough trouble surviving and having even minimal social interaction to have any interest in "fishing". I told myself I would finish the class, but that once it concluded at the end of the year I would not attend the next one. But going home right after church, I was afraid, would only serve to make Sunday afternoons longer. With my depression and anxiety, I had not been able to develop much in the way of interests that I normally pursued. Thinking about this, I wished I was able to teach, but I realized I didn't have the ability to do so in my present condition. However, teachers are always needing more assistants. Perhaps I could assist in one of the classrooms. Inquiring about assisting, I found out that all the classrooms except for 5th grade already had an assistant. They asked if I was interested in assisting with 5th grade. I generally enjoy the younger kids much more than the older ones. However, being able to help anywhere would be an improvement over the adult Sunday School lessons I had been attending. It would be a small step towards getting back to normal. And so I accepted.

As it turned out, Christmas was now over, but the Winter from Hell was just getting started....

A WINTER FROM HELL

While many people consider winter to be their least favorite season, I have always looked forward to winter. As a child growing up in southeastern Virginia, snow was very rare, and as such a big treat. As I got older, I would often lament the lack of snow, particularly during the Christmas season when temperatures would often reach 60 degrees. During and after college I lived in the central part of Virginia. This area had somewhat more snow, but it was often not until February that it occurred. I always longed to live where it snowed more, particularly during the Christmas holiday season. That was part of the reason I moved to Buffalo back in 2000.

Prior to the winter after my brain hemorrhage, I could only recall two times in my life when I did not want to see winter weather. The first was back in late 1990, when I was experiencing severe anxiety and depression related to thyroid problems. I remember visiting my parents at Christmas time, and there was a prediction for mixed winter precipitation later that week. For the first time ever, I told my parents, who thought I would be happy about it, that I honestly didn't want to see this. I had a brain scan scheduled, plus appointments with a psychiatrist, and winter weather would only make those more difficult. The second time I was tired of winter was under more benign conditions. In February 2010, light snowfalls of an inch or two fell for many consecutive days. These snowfall amounts were certainly nothing major by Buffalo standards, but they were enough to snarl traffic during both the morning and evening commutes each day. Worse than that, there was almost no sunshine for several weeks. I remember being tired of winter at that point and wishing for spring.

After several consecutive years of near record warmth, temperatures were close to normal starting in the summer of 2013. I was thankful not to have to deal with hot, muggy weather during my recovery. As fall began, temperatures remained close to normal. This was in sharp contrast to the previous several warm falls. However, nothing seemed amiss during the early fall. In fact, temperatures rose to near 80 degrees during the first weekend during October. If anything, it looked like the record warmth of recent years might be returning. Given my condition, I would not have lamented a mild winter. Like in late 1990, the prospect of a cold and snowy winter did not appeal to me. However, the Buffalo area is well prepared for snow, so I was not particularly concerned about getting to work or doctor's appointments even if it turned out to be a snowy winter.

The first taste of winter came early, on November 11th. Most years, the first accumulating snow does not occur in Buffalo until after Thanksgiving. November 11th was a rare good day for me. In the midst of all my medical issues, anxiety, and depression, I would occasionally (less than once a week at the time) have a day where I felt much better – somewhat close to normal even. Monday November 11th was Veteran's Day – a holiday for many, but not a holiday where I work. I was, however, working remotely from home that day due to the need to attend a church training class early that evening. I remember it had been raining much of the day, and that the rain was predicted to change to snow by early evening. Since church is only about a mile from where I live, I have always walked there and never driven. I was hoping the rain would change to snow in time for my walk to church so I would not have to contend with an umbrella. Sure enough, as darkness fell, some snow began mixing in with the rain. By the time I needed to leave for my walk to church, the precipitation was all snow, though temperatures were still too warm for it to begin accumulating.

Though as mentioned above I was not particularly looking forward to winter this year, I still felt an instinctive mood lift upon seeing the snow. I'm sure it goes back to all the times in the past when I had longed for snow. Even though there is plenty of snow in Buffalo, the first snow is still a treat – assuming I am feeling well enough to enjoy it. That day had been a rare day when I felt better. And now, on a rare good day, I had a chance to enjoy some snow as well. I didn't expect much snow though, aware from past experience that early snows such as this often do not produce much. As I arrived at the church training, several other attendees expressed concern about the snow. "I have to get groceries after the training!", one said. "I hope the roads aren't too bad." Another considered the possibility of her son's school being canceled the next day. "Relax!", I said. "I bet you this snow is over by the time we get out of class." However, snow was still falling when the class ended two hours later. And there was an inch or two on the ground. "Hey, this isn't so bad at all!", I thought to myself as I walked home in the snow. "Maybe the winter I've been somewhat dreading won't be a problem." Little did I know....

The second significant snowfall of the season occurred near Thanksgiving. Once again, it was pretty, and despite the anxiety I was feeling due to my medical issues and the klonopin withdrawal, I found myself feeling better and relaxed as I took a lunchtime walk while working at my job the day after Thanksgiving.

The first week in December saw blustery winds and cold temperatures, but only a dusting of snow. This weather reminded my a lot of what I normally saw during the winter during the six years I lived in the Indianapolis area. My pastor at church is originally from Indiana, and frequently complains about the winters here in Buffalo. Making conversation with him, I asked if he now felt like he was back in Indiana, given the blustery, cold conditions and just dusting amounts of snow. He said "Yeah, this is pretty much like the winter weather we normally get in Indiana."

The second week of December saw more than a half-foot of snow fall, followed by frequent daily snowfalls of an inch or two in subsequent days. Temperatures were more typical of mid-winter than those of December – with highs in the 20s, lows in the teens, and strong winds. Fortunately, much of the snow fell during times when I was not commuting to and from work or doctor's appointments. I wasn't thrilled to see it, given the anxiety and depression I was suffering from, but it was not that big of a deal. After all, it was winter, and what can be expected in winter in Buffalo if not snow? By the end of December, rain had melted all the snow, and things seemed pretty normal for a winter in Buffalo.

Things were far from normal, though, as January 2014 began. After a day off work for New Years on January 1, it was time to return to work on the 2nd. But in Buffalo, a rare blizzard warning was in effect. This was the first time the National Weather Service in Buffalo had issued a blizzard warning in over 30 years. While brief heavy snow squalls are common in Buffalo during the winter, true blizzard conditions are rare. They were last experienced during the winter of 1976-1977, when Buffalo weather made national news headlines every day for several weeks in a row.

Because of the weather conditions, everyone at work was working remotely from home as work began after the holidays. Things only got worse the following week. Temperatures on the morning of January 7th started out in the low teens, and they dropped into the the single digits as the day proceeded. With winds gusting to over 40 miles per hour and heavy snow, visibilities were near zero. Stressed out from the work I was doing from home, I knew I needed to take my usual lunchtime walk. But that day realized the dangers of going outside. The National Weather Service issued warnings advising people to spend as little time outside as possible. I considered staying home – but given my anxiety and the stress from work that day I felt I just had to get out.

I decided to stick to the main road that I live on for my walk for safety reasons. I bundled myself up in my heaviest coat and a hat, and began walking down the road. What surprised me most was that there were almost no cars on the road. Being a main road, with plenty of businesses and stores along the road, normally traffic is heavy at lunchtime. But on that day I would walk for blocks without seeing a car. The few vehicles I did occasionally see were snowplows. As I reached the most distant point on my walk – a shopping center about 1 ½ miles down the road – visibility was just a few hundred feet. Despite being all bundled up, my face was already getting painfully cold. With the low visibility, the road looked unfamiliar, and for a brief moment I began to panic. "Going for a walk today was a pretty stupid thing to do!", I told myself. "What if I were to fall – there's no one to see me – I might freeze to death!", I said. "It's not like I'm 20 years old anymore and I can just ignore the elements! I read about older people being found frozen to death in the winter.", I thought. "Just concentrate on getting back home.", I told myself. My face was painfully cold as I continued to concentrate on putting one foot in front of another walking back towards home. I passed various landmarks – which now looked very different due to the low visibility in the blowing snow – but I realized I was making progress towards getting back home.

Finally, about an hour and 15 minutes after I had left, I was back at my apartment. Normally, that walk would have taken only 45 minutes. Shivering to the bone, I went inside to recover. As it turned out, my face was in fact frost bitten – and for the first time ever, I would experience the dead skin peeling from frostbite in the coming days. But the cold had distracted me from my anxiety about how I felt, and I felt some sense of accomplishment at now having weathered a walk in the most treacherous conditions safely.

The weather that day was to set the tone for the rest of the winter. Though not as severe as this particular storm, every few days a new winter storm would arrive. Strong winds, a half foot or more of snow, and bitter cold temperatures were a fact of life throughout January, February, and even March.

Most days during this time were utterly miserable for me. I had now been incapacitated for the best part of a year. With the anxiety, insomnia, and depression, just surviving work had been my goal. As a result, I had not been able to be proactive about learning new material needed for my work, or about addressing situations and potential problems as they arose at work. Now this was catching up with me. I now had to frequently ask for help from others in understanding and addressing technical issues. Yet these others were often unavailable – due to being too busy or working from home or being out during the work day after having performed implementations the previous night. Much of the time I found myself spinning my wheels. Reiterating my medical issues, I asked my boss to provide as much structure as possible for my work. Yet that fell on deaf ears. With the staff cuts, he didn't have time to oversee anyone's projects properly – much less attempt to make special accommodations for me.

After a stressful and frustrating day at work, I would then often have a grueling commute of an hour or more to get home due to weather conditions. I was always thankful that I managed to get home safely given the extreme weather that often occurred as well as my mental state. But I was also always concerned about what all the stress was doing to my body. On days when the weather was particularly bad, or when I had doctors appointments I needed to attend during the day, I would work from home. Then I would find myself feeling even more isolated from others and lonely, much as had been the case during the late summer when I was working from home all the time. Regardless whether I drove into work or worked from home, by the evening I often felt so stressed and depressed that I could no longer hold back my tears. I would then give myself permission to cry. Usually the crying would has a half hour to an hour, then I would try to move on to more positive things. Unfortunately, the tears seemed to provide little relief, and I would often feel as bad or worse after crying.

The best part of the day for me was the late evening. After doing some flexibility exercises recommended by my doctor for people "as we age", I would have dinner, take a shower, and then participate in the BenzoBuddies forum. Relaxing in this way, and then taking my (decreasing) evening dose of klonopin, I would feel a good deal better by bedtime. Only to get up the next morning feeling bad as ever.

The weather seemed to have a way of interfering at precisely the worst time with whatever I needed to do. If there was an important meeting with my boss at work scheduled for a particular day, it would be the day that everyone had to work from home due to snow or cold. If if was going to snow for just a few hours on a particular day, it would be right during the evening commute home. If I needed to drive a long distance to a doctor's appointment on a particular day, that would be the day it snowed the entire day.

One particular example of the above "Murphy's Law" principle was with the Christian Care and Support classes I was taking at church. These classes met on Monday evenings. I almost never felt like going to these classes after a stressful day, but becoming a Christian Caregiver was something I valued and wanted to make progress on. Of particular emotional difficulty to me were several learning units that dealt with end-of-life and geriatric issues. Reading these made me feel very uncomfortable. Either they would make me feel like I was the one who was now end-of-life (given all the medical issues and other crises I had experienced over recent months), or they would remind me of the situation with my elderly father. I read through the relevant units quickly, and was anxious to get the associated classes out of the way and be able to move on to more pleasant topics. Shortly after I had read through the units on grief, death, and dying in early December, the instructor had become ill and had to postpone the associated class. With the Christmas holidays, these classes were postponed until January. This meant I needed to go through the depressing units once again to review and prepare for the class. I did this. On the day in January when the first class on one of those units was scheduled for that evening, I received a call from the instructor. Due to weather conditions, the class would be postponed. This would mean another week delay, and that I needed to review them material a third time. And what happened the next week – the class was canceled again due to weather, of course. Likewise with the next depressing unit.

A FAITH TESTED

Let me start this chapter out with a few notes added later. As I wrote this chapter originally (in October of 2014), I found myself getting increasingly depressed and upset, because I felt it was portraying people I love and care about (particularly my father) in a very negative light. I realized that the events I described from my childhood and later life made my father, as well as religious leaders and various others in my life, sound tyrannical, selfish, and uncaring. This is not the impression I wanted to give.

My father, and others, definitely made mistakes. But their intentions were good. They did the best they could. It is kind of like with a previous pet cat I had. I tried to give him the best possible care. As it turned out, he ended up dying from a tumor caused by a rabies vaccine that he never needed in the first place, since he was an indoor cat. Getting him rabies vaccines was the wrong thing to do, and he could have lived longer had he not gotten them. But my intentions were good. I did the best I could. Likewise, I remember an incident from my adolescence when I tried to fix something on the garage ceiling and did it by sitting on top of my mother's car. This ended up denting the roof of the car. I had made a mistake, but my intentions had been good. Therefore, I was only reprimanded and not punished for what I had done. I feel that my father, and the others I describe here, were doing the best they could. They were not perfect, but their intentions were good.

It is also important to note that the events that were occurring in the world during the 1960's and 1970s, when much of the referenced material takes place. Since a brain aneurysm can rupture at any age, its quite possible that many readers of this book are too young to have lived through that era. It was the era of the Cold War between the US and the former Soviet Union. Many people in the US at that time were hysterical over the threat of communism, and a lot of people turned to religious fundamentalism. So the ideas and actions of my father were not that much different from those of many other fathers in that era. This was a very anxious time for the US. There was always the threat of a nuclear war between the US and the former Soviet Union. Such a happening could very well have wiped out all life on earth. That threat did not begin to abate until the late 1980's. There was also a lot of social upheaval during that time. There were the race riots of the late 1960's, and the hippie and drug culture of late 1960's and early 1970s. Perhaps the best comparison for the social climate of the 1960s and 1970s for those born later would be the initial years after the 9/11 attacks in 2001. Yet even here, the threat was much less (i.e. little chance of a nuclear war wiping out the world's population), and there were was little in the way of social rebellion like there had been in the 1960s and 1970s.

As a child in the 1960s and 1970s, I grew up up in a home that was very much "old school" when it comes to religion. My mother was the daughter of a Lutheran minister in Iowa. My father grew up in a small, conservative town in Illinois. Both were college-educated, so neither was ignorant as to modern life. We also lived in a major metropolitan area in Virginia – that area presently know as Hampton Roads. So, the traditional, small-town conservatism of my parents was balanced with some degree of modern social views as well. Nevertheless, my parents were very traditional in their interpretation of the Bible and religion.

As a very small child, I remember my mother reading me Bible stories. Those I enjoyed. But I knew I was bored with church. I remember, at about age 4, my mom asking me after she had read me a Bible story "Are you happy when it's time to go to the Lord's house?" I remember wanting to answer no, but saying "yes" because I knew that was what she expected me to say.

My mom was a Sunday School teacher at the church we attended, and in kindergarten I was in her class. She had her ruptured brain aneurysm while teaching me and the rest of the class on February 1, 1970. I still remember seeing what happened. She was holding up a small plastic piggy bank that had something about the Bible on it – I think it was the Ten Commandments. Suddenly, as she was talking, she began to fall forward. The bank flew out of her hands and went bouncing across the room. I remember at first my biggest concern was to go after the bank. Apparently, a teacher in another classroom heard the commotion and came running into the room. She took us to another room. Kids were asking about my mom. I remember the teacher saying that she had fainted, that people faint sometimes and it is not a serious thing. She said that my mom would likely be back the next week teaching. A short while later, I heard loud ambulance sirens. I thought "Someone must have gotten hurt someplace." I didn't associate it with what had just happened with my mom.

It was several long years while my mom recovered. She had a home nurse. My father was very protective of her. I remember getting up early one morning after I thought my father had left for work. I wanted to talk to my mother. Apparently, she was supposed to sleep in late, but I would always go downstairs to talk to her as soon as my father left for work. On that day, my father had not actually left for work yet. I saw him sitting at the kitchen table as I came down the stairs. Shocked, I didn't know what to say. "Are you coming down here to bug your mother?!", he said. "No, I'm not!", I said. "Then why are you coming down here?" "I just felt like going downstairs – uhm – I wanted to watch TV." "You're sure you weren't coming down here to bug your mother?" "Yes, I'm sure." "Well, okay. Remember, your mother is sick. She doesn't need you bugging her."

In the early primary grades, I attended a Baptist school. For whatever reason – perhaps just because I always hated studying history – I despised Bible class. I only ever got one "F" on my report card during my elementary school years. That was in Bible. I remember my mom telling me "In Bible, of all things! That's such a disgrace!" I had quite a few discipline problems in early elementary school. I was frequently sent to the principal's office. I don't remember the exact details, but after a particular misbehavior episode when I was in the 4th grade, my parents took me out of that school and put me in public schools. My father said something like "You don't appreciate being in an air-conditioned, private school. I used to sweat my butt off when I was in school. But now you can go to public school and sweat your butt off like everyone else does!" I remember thinking that I was glad to be out of that school. But I was very concerned about how much I would miss my friends, who I knew I would never see again. I begged to stay for the sake of being with my friends. "You can't act right in a place where you have friends, so I don't have any sympathy for you.", was the response.

Once I was no longer going to the Baptist school, we also stopped attending church there. Instead, we would just listen to a church sermon on the radio every Sunday morning. That was fine with me, since I was growing increasingly resentful of religion. My father listened daily to a "doom and gloom" fundamentalist preacher on the radio. He had my mom tape the sermons during the day, and he would listen to them every evening. Sometimes he would ask me to listen with him. He always seemed to get angry at "Communists" and things happening in the world after listening to such sermons. I didn't know if what the preacher was saying was true or not, but I hated what the sermons were doing to my father, and wanted to have no part in all the negativity. Around that same time, I got a negative impression about "God" in another way. Whenever my father thought I was lying to him about something, he would say "Do you want God to strike you dead if you are lying to me?" I heard this frequently, because I guess I told a lot of lies at the time. I began to question this concept of "God". Who was this "God" person? Was he just some figurehead my father referred to under the threat of being struck dead for lying? I was afraid to talk to my father about this, but occasionally I would mention it to my mother. I found she sided with my father. "Well, people who don't believe in God are the enemy – the Russians, the Communists.", she said. "So you don't want to believe in God? You can go live with the Russians. Kids your age in Russia are not even going to school – they are working." So I didn't know exactly what to think of "God", but I despised having "God" crammed down my throat. I was fully convinced in my own mind that either "God" did not exist, or if he did, he was not the benevolent being I had always heard he was. For me, he was just an excuse for my parents to get on my case. I told my father I no longer wanted to listen to church on the radio. My father accepted me not listening to any of the sermons he listened to during the week, but insisted I continue to listen to church on the radio on Sunday mornings. It was only a half hour a week. For me, it wasn't worth fighting.

My thought of there "not being a God" changed late in my 12th year. It happened totally by chance – it was not anything my parents did. Our family all read the Reader's Digest, which provided, among other things, condensed summaries of recently published books. In early 1977, the Readers Digest did a condensed summary of Ramond Moody's book <u>Life After Life</u>[11]. This was the first widely-read book ever published on near-death experiences. Reading through the experiences of people who had died and been brought back to life, particularly how they saw a benevolent "being of light" and had their life reviewed by this being, rang true with me. The fact that some were able to observe events in their hospital room and even at remote locations while "out of body" and supposedly "dead" convinced me that humans do have a spirit, and that we were made by God. I became very interested in near-death experiences. I kept looking for Raymond Moody's book at the library, but it was always checked out. Eventually, I was able to borrow the book's squeal <u>Reflections on Life After Life</u>[12] from a friend of my father's. After reading the book, I was convinced. But I just filed the information "there is a God" in my mind, and didn't do anything with it. I still had no interest in attending church.

The year before I entered high school, my father made a New Years resolution that he would begin actually attending church again on Sundays, instead of listening

---

[11]   Moody, Raymond A., <u>Life After Life</u>, 1975.
[12]   Moody, Raymond A., <u>Reflections on Life After Life</u>, 1977.

to it on the radio as we had done in recent years. My mom disagreed with something about the church my father chose to attend, so she stayed home and listened to a half-hour sermon on the radio with me. However, before long, my parents resolved the issue of which church to attend, and they both began going together. I stayed home.

When I started high school in the fall, my father said that the following Sunday was "rally day" at church, and that he expected me to attend. I argued with him. He said he wanted me to start attending church each week. After much arguing, we compromised. I agreed to attend church on "alternate weeks". One week I would attend church, and the next week I would stay home – and listen to no sermon at all, radio or elsewhere. So that became my routine my first year in high school. As I continued to attend church on alternate weeks, I was surprised that is was not nearly as bad as I expected. Not only was I now more open to and interested in the concept of "God", after my reading about near-death experiences, but I was also old enough now to follow more of the sermons. This particular pastor was also very laid-back and friendly. I found myself getting interested in the concepts being preached about in his sermons. My father was much surprised when, the following summer, I expressed interest in attending church every week. "I thought this was your week off.", he would say. "Yeah, well its not so bad I guess. Its kind of interesting. I don't mind going.", I said.

From that point on, my faith grew significantly. I attended church regularly, not out of a feeling of obligation, but because I had actually become interested in what was being taught. I started reading through the Bible on my own, completing reading the whole book in a year. With help from my mom, I taught myself the concepts needed to be confirmed at church – instruction I had missed several years earlier when I had refused to take an interest in church. By my senior year in high school, I was studying psychology and had a tremendous interest in child psychology. When I was invited to teach kids at church Sunday School, I jumped at the opportunity to have children to interact with and learn from. That would be the case for many years afterwards in my adulthood as well. While my primary motivation for teaching in the early years was no doubt in order to have a chance to interact with kids, I believed strongly in what I was teaching, and had a strong desire to help others believe it as well.

In my college years, I was one of the few students who actually left the campus and walked to church on Sundays. As in childhood, I never wanted to "go overboard" on church activities. My freshman year a dorm mate tried to get me involved in Campus Crusade for Christ. I told him I did not have time and was not interested. But I did want to attend church weekly to get a perspective on things in my life. In adulthood, I continued to attend church faithfully. But I was very particular about finding a church I was comfortable with. Both when I moved to Indianapolis in 1994, and when I moved to Buffalo in 2000, I attended more than a dozen different churches before I finally settled on one to join. I was not interested in hearing sermons about hellfire and how bad the world situation was, or dry doctrine and intricate details about the life of people in the Bible. I wanted something I could apply during the week. Trying enough different churches, I was able to find what I was looking for. Attending church helped keep me grounded, and helped me make good decisions during the week. At times I let my life get so busy that honestly pretty much the only time I thought of God during the week was during prayer (which I did regularly). Other times I would become interested in a particular adult education class my church was offering, or a particular devotional series, and would think of and stay involved with such things every day.

Early in 2014 (more than 6 months after my brain hemorrhage), I was surprised to find myself becoming somewhat disillusioned with my faith. Though I never seriously doubted the existence of a benevolent God, there were a number of things that caused me to doubt religion as I was presently practicing it.

The first, of course, was the brain aneurysm itself (and the subsequent severe mental symptoms I was continuing to experience). Why would God let that happen to me? How did that serve His purpose? I used to be able to teach Sunday School. Now I could not. How was that helpful? I used to help others at work, but now I took help from them. I used to cheer others up – but now I avoided social interaction because it was too stressful. Instead of me helping my father with his problems, as I had since my mother's death in 1997, now I was relying on him to comfort me by phone whenever our twice weekly calls corresponded with the days I was having the worst symptoms. I hadn't even been able to visit my father in nearly two years – with my spending the time I had last scheduled to visit him in the hospital. I felt guilty about that, even though he assured me that he had no desire to see me in person until my health was better.

The second was a subtle, but to me apparent, accusatory nature I was seeing from the "religious" people I interacted with. First, of course, was my father. "God has been very good to you!", my father would exclaim to me in the weeks after my brain aneurysm. Perhaps it was just me, but I detected a subtle "You now owe God, and if you don't pay him back, he will stop being good to you" tone in these proclamations. While ultimately true that God had been good to me by letting me survive the brain aneurysm and not even experience any physical disability, I still didn't feel real blessed given my ongoing mental symptoms.

When I had requested that the pastor allow my church to be the executor of my will, he had not came through for me. Despite my leaving the church a sizable portion of my estate, he had procrastinated and ultimately dropped the ball, leaving me to scramble to find and executor. And the implication I sensed based on his tone of voice was that my request was "way out in left field". What I sensed – and again this may just have been my anxiety and depression speaking – was "What do you mean you don't have anyone you could list as an executor? God says we are to do things together, not be loners. Why wouldn't you have a dozen different church people who are close friends who could do this for you?" Indeed, a few weeks later, the pastor preached a sermon denouncing the "lone ranger" mentality and saying that God meant for us to do things together. Maybe it was just a coincidence, and maybe I was feeling overly sensitive, but I felt unjustly condemned.

Since I was not able to teach Sunday School, I had attended adult Sunday School classes during the fall of 2013. And I came away unimpressed. The first class topic had been taking responsibility in life. I agreed wholeheartedly with with the theme of personal responsibility, but I had big issues with the way it was presented. The instructor constantly gave examples of how other people – particularly his daughter – did not take responsibility for things. He would complain about her leaving towels on the floor in the bathroom or failing to complete the tasks she had been assigned. I never heard him describe himself learning to take responsibility for things. In that class, I then brought up the topic of my boss. He had been working close to 80 hours a week for over a year in order to compensate for the company failing to hire enough project management resources. In recent months, he had put his foot down, and was now refusing to work more than about 50 hours a week. As a result, myself and other co-workers often did not have the information we needed to complete projects efficiently. Should my boss continue taking responsibility to compensate for the company's ongoing refusal to hire the necessary resources? The answer was "Yes, of course. He could solve the problem if he wanted, right?" It was also implied that I too might be able to compensate for the information I didn't have from my boss if I were also to take responsibility for my own job and put in the appropriate extra hours.

The second topic was evangelism – how it was our duty to bring up the topic of Christianity with our friends and co-workers. I've never been a "salesman". I am very uncomfortable telling others how they should live, whether it be in reference to religion or just life in general. The video series associated with the evangelism topic featured a southern pastor whose mannerisms gave me the creeps. I felt like I was back in my childhood again, being forced against my will to sit in on church sessions that I hated. I knew I didn't want any more adult Sunday School classes, yet I felt (again perhaps it was just me) that I was expected to attend since I was no longer teaching during that time slot.

Likewise, it felt like I was back in the "bad old days" of religion from my childhood when dealing with my father. "Are you reading your Bible?", he would ask. Admittedly, it had been years since I had read my Bible through from cover to cover. I did, however, read a daily Bible devotion each morning. "That's not enough!", he would exclaim. I did have faith in God, but I felt like God was being shoved down my throat again as in childhood. Yet I dared not argue with my father, whose support I needed, nor with the church after all they had done for me during my illness. This was made worse by the way my father would make use of Biblical principals to condemn others. Be they the current politicians, other races, homosexuals, or even just those who do not dress the way he feels is appropriate for church, he frequently had something to condemn.

Because I had seen how helpful it was to me to have someone to take me home from the hospital and drive me to get groceries when I was unable to drive, I had become interested in providing similar care for others. So I was taking training at the church for the Christian Care and Support ministry. This also served as somewhat of a support group for caregivers in general, which I felt would be helpful in my caregiving for my father. Unfortunately, the weekly class meetings tended to be very depressing, and I was becoming disillusioned with the "religious" way some people were handling problems. I have to be vague here because of confidentiality issues. But suffice it to say, one of our senior group participants had a daughter who was having issues with a teacher. Granted, the teacher's morals were horrible – and she deserved to be fired. But this lady was so emphatic about how horrible the teacher situation was with her daughter that her daughter went to her guidance counselor threatening suicide. I doubt the daughter would have taken the situation nearly so seriously if her mother had not presented the teacher situation as such a "horror" to her daughter.

On another occasion, the devotion at the start of one of the caregiving group meetings involved a lesson on "carrying ones cross". In the story chosen for illustration, everyone was complaining to God that their "crosses" (problems) were too big for them to carry (bear). God allowed them, therefore, to put their crosses in a room where they could exchange them for the cross of someone else. When going to select a new cross, everyone saw that the smallest cross in the room full of crosses was their own. Huh? That's saying that everyone's cross was smaller than that of everyone else. Perhaps this story was not meant to be taken literally. But it was unthinking logic such as this that led me doubt the religious activity I was engaged in. In yet another meeting, one of the leaders heard about another bad situation a member's relative was facing. In the prayer he thanked God "that none of us here has been so afflicted". After nearly dying from a brain aneurysm and still facing major symptoms, I felt like saying "Oh, so a brain hemorrhage doesn't count as something serious?"

The final straw that made me admit that I was questioning at least some things about my faith came late in the winter months. On a routine call with my father, he expressed that his arthritis was worsening and that he now felt he should start looking into assisted living. Here I had just gone through a life-threatening brain aneurysm, and had been experiencing severe insomnia, anxiety, depression, and mental disability for over six months. My father was one of the few sources of support I had. Now I needed to support him instead? This was only made worse by my father going over the things I needed to do "when he died", something he had mentioned several times in recent months. "One of my big concerns is the house", I said. What would you want me to do with that? It's probably worth a quarter of a million dollars." "Don't worry about that. It will turn black!", he said. Huh? I had no idea what he was talking about. Finally I got from him that he was concerned about the neighborhood. "It will all be black here in a few years. You don't want anything to do with this house (the house I grew up in....). Sell it right away!" In practically the next breath after this racist comment, he said "Don't worry. God has a plan. He will be with you and show you what to do." At this, I finally said "I don't know. Really, I don't know. I'd like to think that God is with me, but lately I'm starting to doubt." Following that comment, my father went into a long discussion with me about God, as if the fate of my soul was at stake.

In the coming weeks, I thought long and hard about my relationship with God. Had I been wrong all these years? Despite my doubts, I didn't think so. Teachings from the Bible had helped me many times to deal with issues and make good decisions in my life. I was also aware of many times when my prayers were answered. It all made good sense. Those that followed God did better in life than those who ignored spiritual principles. I had seen that play out many times. I also believed the stories of near-death experiencers about what they saw of God. God clearly had a place in my life, and I wasn't about to give up my relationship with him. So then what was it

THE DEVIL AT WORK?

Though at a snail's pace, my health was slowly improving late in the winter. During the worst of my symptoms in the fall, I could expect – if I was lucky – that maybe one day out of six I might feel fairly normal for a few hours in the day. By February, this became say once every three days, and the part of the day where I felt close to my old self expanded from a few hours to a good portion of the day (typically the afternoon and evening). Weaning off the klonopin was helping. Since I was taking less klonopin at night, the anxiety and akathisia I experienced during the following afternoon was less. On February 13th, I took the last klonopin dose, amid much celebration. By that time, I was down to ¼ of a tablet each night.

With training winding down for Christian Care and Support, I now had extra time, particularly on Saturdays. The problem was, because of depression symptoms, working on any of my previous interests seemed to be an oppressive task that just made me feel worse. I could not "lose myself" in hobbies or learning something new like I had been able to prior to my brain aneurysm. The only things that could really hold my attention were things that could help me get better. Fortunately, I've had an interest in psychology for all of my adult life, and reading books on psychology, inspirational books, and self-improvement books was able to provide a distraction to occupy much of my weekends. As I ran across books I might be interested in reading (for example, because they were mentioned in another book I read or I ran across them in the course of searching for medical information for re-assurance), I would note or bookmark them. Then every Friday evening I would pick the book that I most wanted to read and purchase it on Amazon. I would then download it to my Kindle, and read it over the course of the weekend.

During the evenings, I was chatting with females on the Christian Cafe dating service. I had not been on a date or expressed any romantic interests in almost 20 years, being too busy with geeky pursuits. I was still not in any shape to go out on dates, but I did enjoy chatting with women on the Christian Cafe boards. That pursuit occupied a couple of hours of my time on a typical evening.

Throughout the month of February, the weather continued oppressive. Normally in Buffalo during the month of February, only nuisance amounts of snow fall. It might snow half an inch or an inch on most days – but most years there was a break from larger snowfalls until the weather began to get more active again during March. Not so in 2014. Several winter storms with snowfall amounts approaching a foot continued to result in long commutes and needing to work frequently from home.

The period leading up to my brain aneurysm in the spring of 2013 had been when I was acquiring a bunch of lightning detectors. I had over $1000 invested in these. I wanted to put that period behind me, so I planned to sell most of them (keeping just one or two that worked the best). I knew that few people would be interested in buying lightning detectors during the winter, but that interest would increase as spring approached. In late February I listed the detectors on E-Bay. I shipped them off amid a bit of internal celebration the first week in March.

Since early fall, I had not been to a ham club meeting. Besides feeling totally exhausted by evening, weather on the nights of most of the monthly meetings had been an issue, and I didn't feel like driving at night in snowy weather especially given my condition. Now that the weather was beginning to ease and my anxiety continuing to decrease, I wanted to attend the meeting the first Thursday evening in March. After the meeting, the club typically goes to a restaurant to socialize. Unfortunately, I felt I would not be able to go to this because staying out late and then attempting to sleep would severely aggravate my insomnia issues.

The following Saturday, there was also a church planning session that would last from early morning into the early afternoon. Normally, early Saturday morning is when I get groceries. Attempting to go grocery shopping in the

Buffalo area on a Saturday afternoon is likely to be a disaster – both in terms of traffic and crowding/lines in the grocery store.

So I had an idea. It was now a new year, and I again had vacation time at work (after having used all my sick/vacation time in 2013 due to my hospitalization and subsequent doctor visits). I would take Friday (March 7) off work. That way, I could attend the ham club meeting and stay out as late as I wanted on Thursday evening. I would then do my grocery shopping on Friday, which would leave Saturday morning free to attend the church planning meeting. It was a plan.

Unfortunately, things did not go particularly well for my ham club meeting. On Thursday the 6th, I ended up needing to be online for an early work implementation at 5:30AM. As is often the case on days when I need to get up early for work, my sleep the previous night was adversely affected. Because I was taking Friday off and had much stuff to finish, work was also hectic throughout the day on Thursday. By evening, I was quite exhausted and really didn't feel like going to the ham club meeting. Nonetheless, I went. I was glad to get to socialize at the meeting and the dinner afterwards. Even though I didn't feel much like participating, I realized that social interaction was good, and it helped restore some sense of normalcy.

I got home from the meeting and subsequent restaurant gathering at about 11PM, and was in bed by about midnight. Although I didn't sleep particularly poorly, I still found myself awake again by my normal time of getting up at 6AM. I was unable to go back to sleep, so I got up. As a result, I felt tired and a bit anxious throughout the day on Friday. But I went grocery shopping and took care of other errands that I needed to.

Still feeling stressed by Friday night, and with the church planning session impending the next morning, I had a difficult time getting to sleep. I got to bed around 10PM, but it took until after midnight to fall asleep. It was less than an hour later when I was woken up by loud noise. The teen neighbors I had mentioned in an earlier chapter were running around, screaming and in general making a loud racket. Angrily, I pounded on the floor. The noise died down a bit, but it still was far from quiet. I ended up banging on the floor several times more before the night was over. And I could not sleep the entire rest of the night. So on the night before the critical church meeting, after having taken a vacation day from work, I got less than an hour of sleep.

My father always calls me early on Saturday morning. Usually right after we are done talking, I go to the grocery store. On this Saturday, though, I would be walking to church for the planning meeting. I described to my father what I had just gone through the night before. "People have no consideration anymore!", he exclaimed. He then went off into a monologue about declining moral standards. I described how I planned to write a letter to my landlord complaining about the neighbors. "Worse", I said, "I got less than an hour of sleep last night. I wanted to be sharp for the church planning meeting, because that meeting will involve a lot of brainstorming." "It must be the devil at work!", my father exclaimed. He felt that it was the devil that had kept me awake the previous night so that I would give up on going to the church planning meeting. Well, the idea of going to that meeting in my state was about as appealing as going for a root canal, I was nonetheless determined that I would go.

My father continued to talk. "I really need to get going to the church meeting", I told him. Unlike on a typical Saturday when I simply went grocery shopping after our call, I needed to be at church at a set time. Normally, it takes about 15 minutes for me to walk the mile to church. I saw it was only 20 minutes until the meeting was to start. At least this time, there would not be heavy snow to walk through. I could see that there was a dusting of snow on the ground, but that shouldn't slow me down any. I finished the call with my father, put on my coat, and began walking towards church.

But that little dusting of snow, which amounted to less than a quarter of an inch, turned out not to be insignificant. There was a coating of ice under it. Walking down the street, I slipped several times. I tried walking on the grass, but even that had ice and old snow beneath the thin layer of new snow. I had to walk much more carefully and slowly than normal. As I approached the church parking lot, I slipped and fell on my rear end. I yelled some religious words, but they were not put together in a theological manner. I wondered if anyone else, say from the church parking lot, had heard me. When I got up, I saw that one of my pants legs and my rear end was wet with slush and mud.

So I walked into the long-anticipated church planning meeting. A few minutes late. With pants that were wet and muddy. Having gotten less than an hour of sleep the previous night. "How are you doing, Frank?" someone asked. "Are you still sleeping better?" I explained briefly what had happened. I didn't want to lie when people asked me how I was doing (and it was no doubt obvious from the way I looked and acted anyway). It seemed that my answer to that question was always something like "Well, I'm doing a lot better overall – except for today...." I didn't think people believed it. I wasn't even sure I believed it myself sometimes.

Despite the anxiety and sick feeling associated with the lack of sleep, I was able to participate fairly effectively in the brainstorming sessions. I got no sense of accomplishment, and wished I was at home laying down the whole time, but I did participate and provide my input. Shortly after noon, the session concluded. I trudged home. At least the ice was gone. And I set to work at writing the letter of complaint to my landlord....

A PROCEDURE WITH RISKS

I was scheduled for an appointment with my surgeon on Wednesday March 12th. This was to be the one-year followup from my original brain surgery. I had seen my surgeon, neurologist, and other doctors for followup several times over the past year, often preceded by CAT and/or MRA scans. However, this particular visit was of more concern to me. I vaguely remembered that, at one year, it would be necessary to do a followup procedure known as an angiogram. This procedure would involve again invading the brain arteries with a catheter and injecting dye in order to get a good view of the aneurysm to verify that it was still completely closed off. As I vaguely remembered from previous discussions with the surgeon, this procedure requires hospitalization. However, if everything looked good, I would be out of the hospital the same day. Nonetheless, I was understandably nervous about this visit.

There was another complication. My surgeon's office was over 20 miles away from where I live. And as the date approached, weather forecasts were getting worse and worse. Originally it looked like snow for March 12th. As the date got closer, this got upgraded to a winter storm watch, then to a winter storm warning. On March 11th, I was at work. I had not checked the forecast that morning, but I heard a co-worker talking on the phone to a client in another state. "I swear to God, we're supposed to get a foot and a half to two feet of snow from this latest storm!", I heard him say. Nervous, I checked the latest forecast. Not only were snowfall amounts of "1 to 2 feet" predicted, but high wind was also predicted. A rare "blizzard watch" had been issued for the local area.

The evening forecast on March 11th still called for a major winter storm. The saving grace, though, was that snow may not begin until late the following morning. My appointment was for late morning, so I had hope that I could squeeze it in before the weather got too bad. Having just experienced severe insomnia less than a week earlier on the nights before the ham club meeting and church planning session, I expected to have trouble sleeping that night. Surprisingly, though, I slept fairly well. I woke up in the morning happy that I was fairly well rested in preparation for the big day.

Looking out the window, I saw that it was not yet snowing. This was a good sign. Unfortunately, when I checked the weather radar, I saw that snow was right on our doorstep. Indeed, as soon as it got lighter out I saw that snowflakes were already falling. And I could hear the wind picking up. After getting dressed, I logged on to my work computer from home and began responding to E-mail requests.

But I was getting more and more concerned about the weather. Moderate snow was now falling, and strong winds were reducing the visibility to only a couple blocks. To drive over 20 miles to a busy part of town – how early did I need to leave? Maybe as much as two hours early? And conditions were likely to be far worse by the time I made the return trip. A special weather advisory was advising against "unnecessary travel."

As I continued working and pondering what to do, the phone rang. It was my surgeon's office. He was canceling all appointments for the remainder of the day due to the weather. While I felt relieved to hear this, I realized that this would just extend the period of the impending visit, particularly since this surgeon is often booked solid for office visits many weeks in advance. The receptionist asked if I had any preferences for the rescheduled appointment. I told her that my only preference was that it be as soon as possible, to get it over with. I was surprised to get a call back from the receptionist around lunch time. She was able to schedule an appointment for the next day, and was calling to give me the details. I said a prayer of thanks that I would now not have to drive in the storm, and yet I would still know the details of my upcoming surgery soon enough.

Unfortunately, the accumulated stress and the impending appointment took their toll on my sleep that night. Though I had slept fairly well with the impending appointment the night before, I now found that I was unable to sleep. I did fall asleep briefly at times, but would then wake up just minutes later. So on the morning of March 13th, much like the previous Saturday when I was to participate in the church planning session, I was starting the day having had almost no sleep the night before. It seems like this situation was becoming a habit. It is likely that I was still suffering a bit of withdrawal symptoms from the klonopin, which I had finished tapering off of a month earlier. Regardless of the cause, it was quite disheartening.

The snow had stopped, and the sun was out. As I began my work from home, I saw snowplows and snow blowers clearing the parking lot and walkways. I saw that the parking lot was still full – nearly everyone was either working from home that day or waiting for the snow to be cleared before venturing out. I had E-mails from nearly all my co-workers saying that they would be working from home for the day.

Given that it was no longer snowing and winds were no longer strong, I knew that the roads would be fairly clear. Yet my car was still covered in over a foot and a half of snow. I knew I would need time to dig it out. I could also see that the snowplow had piled quite a bit of snow behind my car while clearing the parking lot. I would need time to shovel that as well. So, nearly two hours before the time of my appointment, I logged off of my work computer and went outside to begin clearing away the snow.

The deep snow, my lack of sleep, and the uncertainty associated with my appointment gave the scene an apocalyptic feeling. It felt like I was in the middle of a dream about some terrible disaster that was in progress. We were all trying, in vain, to do what we could to survive. After shoveling away enough snow to get my car door open, I decided to back the car out of the parking space and into the clear area behind it. As I was starting the car and preparing to back up, I heard someone shouting something over the roar of a snow blower. It was the snow blower operator for my apartment building. I could not make out what he was saying. Was he warning me about something? Offering to assist me? "What?", I yelled. He repeated what he had said, but I still could not understand what it was. I turned off the car and walked up to him. Annoyed, he yelled "I was saying, just wait a minute and I'll clear the area behind your car. You don't need to shovel it." "He must think I'm a senile idiot!", I thought to myself.

Roads were clear for most of my drive to my surgeon's office, but traffic was still heavy. I was surprised to see that the parking lot for my surgeon, however, had not been completely cleared. I ended up parking in an adjacent lot. In my tired and nervous state, I was scared that I was going to forget where I had parked, so I made a special effort to note exactly where I was.

The receptionist and nurse both asked how I was doing. I was not going to lie. I told them I had slept hardly at all the previous night. Likewise, when my surgeon called me into his office, I told him the same thing. "One of the problems with any kind of trauma to the brain", he said "is that it can cause insomnia, anxiety, and other nervous conditions." I explained that I had also recently discontinued klonopin, and thought that was part of the issue – along with being nervous about this particular visit.

I had hoped my surgeon would have good news. I had read that, in rare cases, the brain scans provided enough information and followup surgery was not necessary. At a minimum, I wanted to hear re-assurance about the low risks from my followup surgery and how quickly I would be able to leave the hospital. But that's not what I got. "We need to discuss something.", he said. "Sometimes, the initial surgery to close off a ruptured aneurysm is not completely successful. In that case, we need to do additional coiling. And there are some risks with that. I wanted to prepare you for that. You'll need to provide your approval for the additional coiling prior to your exploratory angiogram." I asked him what he meant by "minor risks". "Well", he said, "if we do more coiling there is maybe a two or three percent risk of complications." "What do you mean by 'complications' ", I said. "Well a complication is something bad – you know it could be anything. Like a stroke, other disability...." "You mean I face a several percent risk of another stoke or additional disability from this surgery?", I asked incredulously. "If we end up having to do it, yes.", he said. "And what is the chance that you will have to do additional coiling?", I asked. "I'm not going to speculate on that.", he replied. I asked him what would happen if I didn't have the surgery when it was required. He explained that then I would face a several percent risk per year of additional brain hemorrhaging.

I left the surgeon's office in shock. I had just been through another major winter storm. I had practically no sleep the night before. I was still far from recovered from my original surgery, and now I was to face surgery again, along with additional risks? I didn't know how much more of this I could take.

I got home earlier than I had expected. Rather than get right back to work, I sat around thinking. I was scared. I was demoralized. I began crying. After about a half hour, I pulled myself together. I had promised my father I would call him and let him know the results of my doctor visit. I dialed his number. I explained what had transpired – the snow, the lack of sleep, my surgeon's news. "Tell God you are scared and don't know what decision to make. He will help you.", said my father. Well, I did know what my decision had to be. If additional coiling was needed, I had to get that done, since that was far less risky than facing a several percent chance of additional brain bleeding each year.

I logged back on to my work computer and wrote an E-mail to my boss. I told him I felt devastated. Still far from recovered from my first surgery, I now faced surgery again. And it might mean another lengthy stay in the hospital. He needed to know that for planning purposes. I got no reply. Instead, I soon got a notice that there was an emergency client conference scheduled to start in about an hour to discuss a production issue that had just come up. "Oh, for heaven's sake", I thought. "Just what I need, another crisis. And how am I possibly going to be able to think clearly to respond to the client's questions given my lack of sleep and what I just went through with my surgeon?" I began to feel resentful. "Why am I knocking myself out to work when I face so many problems", I asked myself. "Why didn't I just go on disability for a while to give myself proper time to recover? That's why I pay the big bucks for disability coverage!" I realized I had came back to work far more quickly than others who had similar medical issues. That was my own choosing – I wanted something to distract myself from what I had just gone through. But with the prospect for additional surgery and more risks, I began to think I had made a serious mistake.

PART-TIME WORK

Pending the results of several medical tests that are routinely done prior to major surgery, my surgery was scheduled for 6AM on April 9th. I was given instructions to arrive two hours early, and not eat anything after dinner the previous evening. The instructions also stated that I would not be able to drive until I was re-evaluated at a followup appointment approximately two weeks after the surgery. I was warned that I could face several days of hospital recovery, and of course there was the small risk of major complications.

Though I mostly got over my initial panic about the situation within a couple days, I was still feeling quite distraught. Nearly a year after my brain aneurysm, I was in worse mental shape than when I had left the hospital. The thought of now having another procedure when I was still far from recovered seemed almost unbearable. Then there were the practical aspects to consider. I would need someone to take me to the hospital at 4AM. I would need to take time off work for my hospitalization, then would once again be back to working from home. Already feeling isolated by my illness, I was dreading that. And, I didn't have any more sick time left at work, having taken three weeks of sick week the previous year for my initial hospitalization and having used all my vacation time for follow-up appointments and medical tests. I had not seen my aging father, who was now having health issues with arthritis, nor taken any other vacation in nearly two years. The thought of again using up vacation time for medical issues did not appeal to me at all. I was going to have to take unpaid time.

Given the mental issues I was facing and my lack of sick time, my surgeon made the suggestion that I work part time. I felt bad about this. It would seem like I was not getting better, but instead getting worse. Yet thinking it over, I realized this is what I needed to do. It was more important that I be able to rest, and have vacation time available to see my father and friends, than it was to make my full salary, or to pretend that everything was normal. We discussed and agreed that a goal of 32 hours of work a week (instead of the normal 40) would be reasonable. Fortunately, I have always been quite conservative with my finances. I live well below my means. I did some calculations and determined that I would be able to live on 4/5 of my salary without too many issues.

Looking back over the past year since my stoke, I could see that work had not been particularly kind to me. About once a week, there were production implementations at 5AM. These often worsened my insomnia on the night before. Worse, my company had lost two managers over the past year, and had not replaced them. This left my boss/manager unable to manage my projects effectively. Double and sometimes triple booked in meetings throughout the day, it was very difficult to get time with him if I had questions about a project or other issues. If I did get time with him, he was almost always distracted – responding every minute or two to chat messages or urgent E-mails, or having someone else with an urgent issue poke their head into his office. E-mailing was not very effective either – his E-mail inbox continually showed thousands of unread messages.

When I was in the hospital for three weeks and it was not even known for sure whether I would survive or not, my boss had assigned all the major projects I had been working on to others. When I returned to work, things were still quite uncertain about my availability. So my boss assigned me to all legacy projects. Unfortunately, the people who had developed the legacy applications initially had now moved on and had little or no time to assist me with questions. The company sees legacy support as having less of a priority than work for new clients, and given their resource shortage they were not willing to pull anyone off the new projects to assist me with questions about legacy framework and applications. So I was pretty much on my own – something that I found quite stressful in my condition. Likewise, the machines and infrastructure that support legacy development were in quite poor shape due to the company not giving it as much priority as that supporting new clients. Thus a significant portion of my time was spent getting around machine problems instead of working on the tasks I had been assigned. This combined with my anxiety and lack of mental clarity to make work quite stressful for me.

I really wanted to leave my present job given the things that were going on there. But I certainly was in no shape to find another job at that point, particularly a software development job that was part-time. Nor would I want to take a chance in changing insurance coverage with my medical condition uncertain. So instead, I worked on consoling myself and finding positive things about my job to think about. There were several. Overtime was very rare, which certainly is not the case for all jobs of the type, so I was thankful for this. I could know that, regardless how difficult things were, I only had to survive until 5:30 and then I would be able to go home and relax. Likewise, getting called unexpectedly outside work hours due to production issues was very rare. Having once worked at a company where I would get called multiple evenings a week and sometimes even in the middle of the night with production issues that had to be solved right away, I appreciated the certainty of knowing that once I was home, my work was done for the day and I didn't have to think about it until the next day. Another big positive was that my company was very reasonable when things went wrong. If someone such as myself was unable to accomplish something in the allocated time due to unforeseen issues, or they had tried their best but made an honest mistake, this was never held against them. Finally, I knew that my job was secure, or at least as secure as possible in my industry today. With

you. 32 hours a week is almost full-time. I'll do my part to organize things so that you can work as efficiently as possible during the time you are here. The first thing I'm going to do is take you off of all client-facing conference calls. That should save a few hours a week. You can concentrate on your primary role – software development...." My heart sank. I knew I might well need to work from home for two weeks or more. When I had needed to work from home after getting home from the hospital the previous year, client calls had been the main thing that helped me to feel less isolated and lonely. Now even this was going to be taken away. But, what could I say?

I did feel better though now that things were finalized. My boss knew my surgery schedule, even if the length was uncertain, and he could plan around it. Working part time, I knew I would be able to take vacation to visit my father and various friends during the summer, and I could start planning and looking forward to that.

NOT MY IMAGINATION

I never did much research on subarachnoid hemorrhage when I got out of the hospital. I knew the basics from what the doctors told me. I knew the grim statistics – that one in three die, one in three experience significant disability, and one in three have no serious lasting effects. But when I got out of the hospital in May 2013, I didn't want to dwell on this and scare myself unnecessarily. It was obvious that I was still alive, so I was not part of the first third. With the exception of the complications from the surgery itself that required me to walk with a cane for a short period, there was no disability. My mental abilities were still intact. So I must be in the third group. Doctors assured me that, once out of danger from the original hemorrhage, the chances of experiencing another in my lifetime were quite small – on the order of 15%[13]. As I overcame the physical disability caused by the blood

---

[13] "What You Should Know About Cerebral Aneurysms", American Stroke Association, http://www.strokeassociation. org/STROKEORG/AboutStroke/TypesofStroke/ HemorrhagicBleeds/What-You-Should-Know-About-Cerebral-Aneurysms_UCM_310103_Article.jsp#.

clot in my leg from the surgery, I was certain that I was in the third group. Why did I need to research any further? What I needed to do, if anything, was to make up for lost time. I had missed several weeks of work, so I had catching up to do there. Plus I would be missing more for followup appointments. And now more aware of my own mortality, I had plenty of things I needed to do in my life as well. There was no time for dwelling on what had happened.

I didn't realize it at the time, but I was not in the third group. I was in the second group. That would become painfully obvious over the coming months. The idea of delayed effects never occurred to me. As I experienced insomnia, anxiety, and depression in the coming months, I assumed that this was just PTSD re-activating my past episodes of anxiety and depression. And to some extent that is true. But further research has shown me that some the effects are likely the physical effects of brain trauma.

With the revelation that I again faced surgery risks, I finally decided to research brain aneurysms in March 2014. Having been helped very much by support in the BenzoBuddies forum as I worked to get off of klonopin, I decided to check out some support forums specifically dedicated to brain aneurysms[14][15]. As I read these forums, I began to see a familiar pattern. People described how

---

[14] Brain Aneurysm Support Community, http://www.bafsupport.org/.
[15] Neurotalk Support Community, http://neurotalk.psychcentral.com/.

they had been okay initially, but gradually developed mental symptoms. Difficulty concentrating, extreme irritability, depression, anxiety – these all sounded like my symptoms. Most of the information online about strokes concentrated on damage to specific areas of the brain caused by the stroke. I knew it was unlikely, based on the location of the aneurysm itself, the initial lack of mental symptoms, and the fact that the symptoms now would go away from time to time – that the effects I was experiencing were caused by damage to a specific area of the brain. However, someone in one of the forums mentioned how the brain can be affected in general by trauma. They recommended researching traumatic brain injury for information about the mental effects many survivors face.

I didn't have to go far to research this. I found out that a co-worker had suffered traumatic brain injury as a young man as the result of an industrial accident. He was able to describe the accident and the events immediately following, but said there was a several-month period starting a few weeks later that he was having severe mental issues that he could barely remember. He had to go back to living with his parents temporarily at that time. He also described issues with extreme irritability, difficulty concentrating, and migraine headaches that continue (to a much lesser extent) to this day. Describing the time he spent living his parents after the accident, he said "I don't remember hardly anything about what I was like during that time – but my parents tell me I was a total jerk!"

My online research on traumatic brain injury provided further confirmation that the symptoms I had been experiencing were not purely psychological. According to the Mayo Clinic[16], the symptoms following a brain injury include the following: headaches, dizziness, fatigue, irritability, anxiety, insomnia, loss of concentration and memory, and noise and light sensitivity. I had experienced many of these symptoms over the past year – basically everything except for the headaches and dizziness. In a way, this was comforting, because it showed that the effects were not (at least completely) psychological. On the other hand, it didn't make things any better as far as my condition. There were no quick cures. In general, most people experience a slow improvement with time – but the duration is highly variable.

As the date of my surgery approached, I grew more nervous. With a chance, though small, or significant complications, I give someone from church Power of Attorney if required. The act of doing this almost made it seem imminent, though my logical mind knows that the chances of needing to use this are quite small. I also send out an Email to everyone in my department at work describing in general terms the problems I have faced over the past year, my upcoming surgery, and plans for working part-time afterwards. Although everyone in my department was well aware that I had experienced

---

[16] "Traumatic Brain Injury – Symptoms", Mayo Clinic, http://www.mayoclinic.org/diseases-conditions/traumatic-brain-injury/basics/symptoms/con-20029302.

a ruptured brain aneurysm, many were not aware of the ongoing issues I was experiencing. After all, I looked completely normal, and was working normal hours. Based on experience from past episodes of anxiety and depression, I was never one to go around complaining to others about symptoms – doing so would only serve to magnify the symptoms and alienate those around me. Plus, I was always busy trying to keep up with my work given my concentration difficulties so had little time for chit-chat. And my anxiety had resulted in an almost phobic social avoidance for a good portion of the time since my hospitalization. In addition, a significant portion of my co-workers live in other cities and work remotely. The only time I talk with them is on conference calls with clients, so they have little interaction with me. Though I did not go into a lot of details on the specifics, I described in the E-mail my condition in general terms. I did receive a fair amount of support from others who read the E-mail. A couple replied that they had in fact noticed that I seemed stressed since my brain hemorrhage, and they commended my decision to reduce my working hours from 40 to 32.

As had been the case several times over the previous month on the night before a major event, I slept only a couple of hours the night before my April 9th surgery. I was already awake when my alarm went off at 4:30AM. My ride picked me up around 5:15AM. We went to the hospital, and I checked in. I was sent to a waiting area, being told that I would be taken to the surgery preparation once my surgeon arrived. After waiting nearly an hour and still no one had came to get me, I called the hospital using the phone in the waiting room. They told me that my surgeon had just arrived, and that some one would come to get me shortly.

In the surgery preparation room, I was told to undress and get into the hospital gown. A nurse started two IVs – one in my left arm and one in my right arm. This was to be in addition to the site where the surgeon would enter a main artery in my groin area. The nurses and assistants all asked how I was feeling, which unfortunately was not very good after my lack of sleep the night before. I overheard two nursing assistants discussing the vacation one had recently taken to Montego Bay. Their happy talk only made me feel isolated. It must be nice, I thought, to be able to enjoy oneself on vacation instead of having to worry about surgery and growing older, I thought, as an assistant fitted me with a urine catheter.

My surgeon wheeled me on a stretcher into the surgery room – a room with high ceilings and full of machines that reminded me of an auto repair garage. After my experience with addiction to klonopin, I listed "benzodiazepines" as an allergy on the admission form and explained that I would prefer not to have any benzos administered as part of the surgery unless absolutely necessary. The anesthesiologist acknowledged my wishes, saying he planned to give me a non-benzo sedative.

The surgery began with the assistant surgeon creating an incision in my groin area where a catheter could be inserted. Slowly, the catheter made its way towards my brain. I didn't feel anything significant, other than the sedative effects of the drug I was being given with one of the IVs. Once the catheter reached the brain, the doctors warned me that they were going to be injecting dye – and that this dye would make my face flush. I felt the flush. The surgeon and his assistant continued to look at a picture of my brain on a large screen in the operating room.

"You can go ahead and inform the patient", I heard my surgeon say to his assistant. I waited with baited breath to hear what he had to say. "Everything is fine.", the assistant said. "No coiling is required. We'll be done here in just a few more minutes." I breathed a sigh of relief.

I was wheeled to the recovery room. Looking at the records of what was done, nurses kept asking my why there was no coiling. I explained that none was required. "That's a good thing!", they would say. I agreed. Later my surgeon came in to discuss the surgery results. He explained that originally, the brain scans had shown blood flow still occurring in an area that should have been stopped by the original coiling. However, this had turned out to be a false indication, due to the angle at which the scans had been done and the location of the aneurysm. The vessels that had blood flowing, in fact, should have had blood flowing. "So how does the future look then?", I asked my surgeon. In a somewhat joking manner, he replied "Future? For you, very good. For me – I don't know." I felt relieved. "We'll do another scan at a year, then maybe at two year intervals after that.", he said.

A nurse said that they would soon have someone remove the urine catheter. They planned to keep me in the recovery room for a few hours of observation, then send me home. I texted the good news to the friend who had given me a ride. I knew she was working and would not be able to take me home until that evening, but I wanted to share the news anyway. I sent an E-mail to my pastor and others at church describing the outcome. I E-mailed my cat sitter to let her know that I would be out of the hospital that day, and would not need any further pet sitting services after that day. Soon the hospital brought me lunch. Having not eaten since dinner the previous day, I was actually hungry despite still feeling exhausted and emotionally drained.

I was released early that evening with instructions to "take it easy" for a couple of days, but other than that, no restrictions on activities. And the biggest good news was that I was able to drive. I wouldn't have work from home or rely on my stash of groceries after all.

As I arrived home, I saw that my apartment was having a new roof installed. Despite the fact that is was evening, the work was still going on. A note from my cat sitter said that when she had visited, my cat Patrick had spent pretty much the whole time hiding under the bed due to all the noise. As I talked with my father on the phone to let him know how surgery had went and that I was now home safely, loud pounding could be heard. My nerves were still on edge from the lack of sleep and the surgery. I was dismayed that I would now be spending a couple of days stuck in my room listening to all the noise from the new roof being installed while resting and recovering. Still, it did not seem to be such a big deal in the overall scheme of things. I concentrated on the good news regarding my surgery.

I slept much better that night, and the nights following. I mostly read and rested in bed the following day. The day after that, I took my car into the shop for routine service, but spent the rest of the day reading and resting. By Saturday (3 days after my surgery), the effects of the surgery had all faded. The following Monday, I returned to work (now part time).

My slow recovery, which had been interrupted by my surgery, began to progress again. One of the first things I did, with the uncertainty of the surgery now behind me, was to request time off from work and purchase plane tickets to visit my father in early May. I could also now turn my efforts to other aspects of recovery. The shorter work hours allowed me extra time for walking, as well as for meditating twice a day. With the Christian Care training now completed, I no longer had (often) depressing material I needed to read on the weekends. Now that I was finally sleeping better again after my struggle with klonopin, I saw no reason to continue spending time on the BenzoBuddies support forum each evening. I still had little to no interest in technical things, but I knew I needed to concentrate on some sort of goal to help keep my mind off continued mental symptoms. I turned to reading psychology and self-improvement books, reading one or more complete books a week

I began writing about my brain aneurysm experience. I had gotten the idea to write a book shortly after I learned that I would face surgery again. I had been helped by learning from books by benzodiazepine survivors. I knew that writing about my experience might be helpful and re-assuring for others. It would also help me better integrate and move beyond my experience. In a flash of inspiration just a few days after my surgery, I sat down and came up with the titles of nearly all the chapters I wanted to include in my book. I only made slight changes and a few small additions in the months that followed as I wrote the book.

Over the next two months, I felt better. I was still far from normal mentally. Some days I still experienced major anxiety and depression. But now I would have whole days at a time, sometimes even two days in a row, where I felt fairly close to my "old self". On those days in particular, I was able to enjoy my reading. Some days I was even able to enjoy my work to some extent, and even had some minor technical interests at home.

I reviewed my progress over the year since my initial hospitalization. During the summer, I had been unable to sleep some nights. Klonopin had helped with sleep, but by fall I had experienced anxiety so severe that it almost became a phobia when it came to social situation and new experiences. Depression also became a serious problem while on the klonopin. Just occasionally – perhaps one day out of six – I might feel better and somewhat like my "old self" for a few hours before bedtime in the evening. As I began slowly cutting down on the klonopin starting in late November, I would now sometimes experience better - "near normal" feeling for larger portions of the day – sometimes even the majority of the day – about one day out of six. This was at the expense of having more sleep issues again. By May (a year after my hospitalization), out of three days, on average, I would have one "good" day where I felt close to my "old self" for most of the day. One day I would feel less well, but still better than at the worst of my illness. And one day of the three would still be bad. But even on those days, in most cases, I was still able to concentrate fairly well and accomplish the things I needed to at work and at home. And sleep issues had now become rare.

Besides the ongoing mental issues, I still had a lot of problems to face though. Seeing my father for the first time in a year and a half was not an uplifting experience, as much of my time and discussion with him centered on making arrangements for his eventual assisted living. As mentioned earlier, my lot at work had deteriorated significantly as my illness prevented me from being as proactive about problems as I normally am. Still, dealing with external issues was certainly progress over dealing almost exclusively with my own health issues.

THE AORTIC VALVE IS BI-CUSPID

The above chapter title is what I wrote in my diary for June 17th. In the long process of trying to take back my life, there would be yet another concern added.

In preparation for my second surgery in April, routine tests were done to locate any potential issues that might interfere with the surgery. Because of the emergency nature of the first surgery, there was no time for these tests. But for the "routine" second surgery, plenty of tests were done. These tests included a chest X-ray and other cardiac tests. During the course of these routine tests, an abnormality in my heart was discovered. It was not serious enough to affect the surgery, but nonetheless it was noted in my medical record.

When I visited my primary care doctor in June for an annual checkup, he mentioned this entry in my record. "It says here that that there is mild to moderate regurgitation in your aorta. That's something we should follow up on. I'm going to schedule you for a cardiac ultrasound." Regurgitation? Huh? I was dumbfounded. I tried to get more information from my doctor, but he was vague. "It's something some people have. It may or may not be serious. We'll know more after the ultrasound." Great. Another thing to worry about.

I had the heart ultrasound test on June 16th. On June 17th, I had an online message from my doctor describing the test results. Here is an excerpt: "The aortic valve is bicuspid. There is mild aortic valve sclerosis without stenosis. There is mild-to-moderate aortic regurgitation. This is minimal aortic root dilatation, 3.9 cm this time, less than 4. But the CTA should be done. I ordered this. Please call or E-Mail the office to set this up".

So, another test – this time a CT scan, with dye, of the heart region. On June 23rd, I had the CT scan. The results indicated a moderate, though not yet dangerous, aneurysm of the root aorta. Via E-mail, I discuss the results with my doctor. He explains that having a bicuspid aortic valve is a congenital (birth) defect, affecting 1 to 2 percent of the population. The majority of people born with this defect require heart surgery at some point in their life. The time at which this surgery is required can range from right at birth, all the way up to old age. In my case, there is no immediate threat, but this is something that will need to be monitored. My doctor sets up an appointment with a cardiac specialist for an initial baseline consultation. Because it is not an emergency, this appointment is not available for nearly two months.

This information does calm my fears quite a bit. I begin researching just what a "bicuspid aortic valve" is. It is a congenital defect – something that is present from birth, though often not diagnosed until later in life. One to two percent of the population have this, with it being about twice as common in males as in females[17]. In my research, I run across an amazing fact. A bi-cuspid aortic valve indicates a general disorder in the blood vessel system of the body. People born with a bi-cuspid aortic valve are **ten times** more likely to have a brain aneurysm than the general public[18].

So that helps explain why I had a brain aneurysm. I didn't have the typical lifestyle risks that are generally associated with brain aneurysms (high blood pressure, smoking, excessive alcohol use, use of strong stimulants such as cocaine). But I was born with a bi-cuspid aortic valve. It was never diagnosed, but it had been with me all my life.

My visit with the cardiac specialist on July 25th was re-assuring. While my condition will need to be monitored on a regular (probably yearly) basis, there are no major contraindicated activities. I'm free to engage in strenuous activities, including running. The only thing

---

[17] "Bicuspid Aortic Valve Disease", Cleveland Clinic, http://my.clevelandclinic.org/services/heart/disorders/valve/bicuspid_aortic_valve_disease.

[18] Neurology, American Academy of Neurology, April 4, 2010, As reported by Science Daily, http://www.sciencedaily.com/releases/2010/05/100503161227.htm.

I am advised against doing is heavy workouts using weights. I remember in my high school days working with weights in the gym. It was one of my least favorite forms of exercise. I had not done it since.

In August, I had a followup appointment with the neurologist who had initially treated my brain aneurysm. The followup tests of physical abilities indicated that there was still no impairment. With that, my neurologist said that I would no longer need to see him again on a regular basis. I was all clear. It would mean one less series of doctor appointments.

So gradually, over the course of the spring and summer, I began to lose the worries about physical aspects of my condition, for the first time since my brain aneurysm more than a year earlier. It had happened in steps, with big setbacks along the way. First there had been the year followup surgery and associated risks. That had turned out well, and my research now indicated less than a 10% lifetime risk of additional aneurysm complications or future surgeries. Then there had the bi-cuspid aortic valve concerns. While still a general concern, there was no immediate danger with this. I no longer needed to see the neurologist on a regular basis, because the risks related to my initial brain aneurysm were now over. So by later in the summer, my concerns were almost solely about continuing mental issues, which were unfortunately still quite prevalent and producing significant anguish and disability.

SLOWLY TAKING BACK MY LIFE

Following my second surgery in April 2014, I slowly began taking back my life. For the first year after my brain aneurysm, I had no life. Life was just a matter of survival. Following the second surgery and after I had gotten over my klonopin addiction, I began to slowly have a life again. It's been a long, hard process, and to this day (November, 2014), I am still experiencing significant issues. But the overall trend has definitely been up, and now I have a fair number of days when I feel pretty much like my "old self", with interests and enjoyment of life.

I continued to read books on psychology and how to deal with stress and adversity, reading an average of one book a week during the spring and summer. One new technique that greatly assisted in my recovery process was Acceptance and Commitment Therapy (ACT)[19]. ACT consists of 6 key psychological skills. Two of the skills that I found particularly helpful are Values and Committed

---

[19] See Bibliography entry for Hayes and Wilson.

Action. "Frank" as a person hardly existed during the first year after my brain hemorrhage. My "values" consisted of just trying to survive. I did not express my opinions openly about anything, even if it directly affected me. For example, when I was dissatisfied with something happening at work, I said nothing. I didn't want to put myself up for possible scrutiny by "rocking the boat", given that was dependent on my boss and others at work "liking" me given my reduced abilities. I would accept all sorts of crap – lack of project management, lack of proper equipment and environments for developing and testing, continual assignment to "drudgery" tasks where I had little autonomy, etc. I felt like I "owed" this to my employer, given what the accommodations they had made and were making for my illness. The same held true with issues and things that bothered me about the Christian Care and Support ministry I had become involved with a church. And even in conversations with my father, who likes to argue politics, I no longer really had a position. I just tried to get along.

The ACT books talked about how we can get so caught up trying to survive it takes up our whole life. We no longer have other values and goals, and this feeds back into a loop of more depression and anxiety. One of the first things I did late in the spring was to sit down and clarify my values. In thinking about it, my values had changed quite a bit. I no longer valued, or enjoyed, staying busy with a bunch of technical hobbies. But I had other values besides that. I was able to list these values, and then start working on some goals related to them.

Trying to distract myself and "feel better" by engaging in random activities I hoped I would enjoy had not been very motivating over the past year. But when my activities were in pursuit of things related to my values, I had motivation to continue for the sake of the goals/values, even if I was not enjoying the process at the time. This helped keep me more engaged in life, and gave me, to some extent, a feeling of accomplishment.

Attempts at doing "normal" things again had mixed results. In May, for example, I visited my father for the first time in nearly two years. His biggest need at that point was for me to assist him with his choice of a future assisted living facility. Visiting various care facilities with him and researching information on this topic online was depressing. Yet I could take some consolation in the fact that this was in service of one of my values "helping my father adjust to old age". I felt bad much of the time during the visit. Yet I was able to enjoy an evening with an old friend from high school. This was in support of my value of "spending more time with friends".

Some things went unexpectedly well. These surprises made life seem good and fun again, at least while they lasted, and gave me increasing hope for the future. For example, one of the values I listed is doing work that I enjoy. I could see that my job had been steadily moving away from that, particularly in the past couple years. While I knew it would be unwise to change jobs and insurance in the middle of my medical and mental issues, I could at least start taking steps in that direction.

I also realized that the values that had brought me to the Buffalo area back in 2000 had evolved and changed. Buffalo was likely no longer the best place for me to live. Again, I was not prepared to move anytime real soon. But I could at least start considering what other cities I would like to live in, and begin looking at the job market in these cities.

In early June, I decided to visit Columbus, Ohio, as that seemed to be a place I might want to move to once my medical issues were resolved. Soon after I checked into my motel room there, I turned on a ham radio receiver. I wanted to hear ham radio operators talking to learn more about what people in Columbus were like. Less than five minutes after I turned on the radio, I heard a voice that sounded familiar. Sure enough, one of the people taking was an old ham friend who I had talked to almost every day back in the late 1990s when I lived in the Indianapolis area. On this trip, I had only planned to listen to hams communicating and not talk myself, so I only had a receiver and not a transmitter with me. However, I realized that I had a transmitter in my car that I could use. I rushed to my car and frantically worked to program in the channel information needed to transmit on this frequency, all the while my friend saying that he was in his car and almost to his destination. I managed to complete the programming just before he signed off, and was able to catch him. It turned out he was still living in Indiana, but was doing a temporary job in the Columbus area. We ended up having dinner together and talking about old times in Indianapolis.

One good thing can lead to another. My old friend was a former Navy seal. Though we never discussed my medical issues at all (I did not bring up the topic), I was struck by his "can do" attitude towards problems in general – something I had not seen in a while. This caused me to get interested in the psychological fitness training that Navy seals do. I figured I could learn from this psychological fitness training to better handle my remaining issues. So I read a couple of books on Seal training. These books were helpful to me, and gave me goals for psychological growth.

In keeping with my value of spending more time with friends, I visited other old friends during the summer. I spent two days with an uncle in Wisconsin I had not seen since childhood, and spent a day with an old friend who I had met at work when I first moved to Buffalo but who had moved to Chicago a few years ago. Valuing relaxing instead of always trying to "accomplish something" (as with storm chasing, for example) on vacations, I also spent a couple of days on the beach in Florida. I had not been to the beach since college.

What I found as I traveled was that my enjoyment of the activities was dependent on my mental state. I continued to experience big fluctuations in my mental state. A typical pattern went like this. On a particular day, I would experience some degree of anxiety and depression. I would be able to distract myself somewhat by concentrating on what I was doing, but it would always come back. I could continue doing whatever activities

I happened to be doing though without significant problems. If I interacted with others, they could not tell that anything was wrong. Typically on the next day, symptoms would worsen. Anxiety and depression were very noticeable, and even interfered somewhat with my ability do desired activities. I could get through my activities, but others I interacted with could sense my anxiety and low mood. Then – often late that evening – I would start to feel better. The following day, there would be almost no anxiety or depression. I would be my "old self". Then things would start deteriorating again the following day. I found that this pattern continued to apply even when I was relaxing on vacations. It was not always exactly three days long – it varied in length despite always adhering to the same basic pattern. So I could not generally plan to take advantage of "good" days or avoid things on "bad" days. When I was lucky enough to have the "good" days occur in sync with visits to friends or other fun activities, I greatly enjoyed them. At other times, I would just be there and interact with my friends or do the activities I had planned, but it was mainly just going through the motions.

I do not know the cause of the big mood swings. Was it the physical trauma to the brain from the hemorrhage? Was it psychological stress from my illness and new age-related issues re-activating past instances of anxiety and depression? One thing I became suspicious of was the fluoxetine (prozac) I had been taking for more than 12 years. With my past history of multiple depressive episodes, my psychiatrist had recommended that I stay on

Prozac "for life" in 2001. I had not had any major anxiety or depression symptoms since then (prior to my brain aneurysm). Yet I wondered – was this drug really effective in the long term? Were there studies of this? How did I know that, like with the klonopin which helped for a short time but made things far worse in the long term, the fluoxetine was not making things worse? I did some research, and read about a phenomenon called "prozac poop out" that often occurs when taking antidepressants long-term[20]. As it turned out, there were no studies that showed the long-term efficacy of taking antidepressants. Indeed, just the opposite appeared to be true. Just like the brain adapts to benzodiazepine tranquilizers with compensating changes that leave the patient worse off in the long term. I had experienced that with klonopin. Patients who take antidepressants long-term often find that they stop working after a few years. At that point, the dose is often increased, or another antidepressant is added. Increased dosage and the addition of another medicine often produce their own side effects, which then are treated by adding yet another drug. This process can often continue to the point where the patient taking a cocktail of psychiatric drugs and end up disabled[21].

I did much research on how to taper off antidepressants. I learned that it is best to take a month for every year one

---

[20] "Tarditive Dysphoria: The Role of Long-Term Antidepressant Use in Inducing Chronic Dysphoria", Medical Hypotheses 76 (2001) 769-773, http://www.toxicpsychiatry.com/storage/antidep%20 El-Mallakh-tardivedysphoriadarticle1.pdf.

[21] See Whitaker, Robert in Bibliography.

has been on antidepressants to get off of them. Having been on prozac for more than twelve years, I knew I would need to take a year or so to get off of it. Prozac has a very long half-life, so one way to taper is to start skipping more and more days while taking it. I decided this was what I was going to do. In March 2014, I began skipping taking the prozac one day a week (Sundays). Then in May, I added a second day (Monday). Then I added Tuesday in July, and Wednesday in September. By late November, I was only taking prozac two days a week (Friday and Saturday). The plan is to start taking it only on Saturdays starting in January, and then to stop taking it entirely in March.

As with tapering off klonopin, tapering off prozac is definitely making things worse in the short term. Looking at previous diary entries, I see that the same thing happened before when discontinuing prozac. After my first treated depression in 1990, my doctor had me discontinue prozac in June of 1991. Although I did not realize the cause at the time, I see from diary entries a low period in the fall and early winter of 1991. Likewise, my doctor had me discontinue prozac in July 1998, after two years of treatment. I experienced significant issues with depression and sleep during the fall of 1998 – in fact, even consulting my doctor – but got through them and recovered completely by early 1999.

As I have been skipping more and more days taking prozac, I have noticed my symptoms generally beginning to line up with days of the week. Starting in August (when I was skipping 3 days), I have noticed increasing anxiety and depression on the first days I skip (Sunday and Monday). In fact, going back to September (now more than two months), I have not had a single average or better Sunday. A typical present pattern goes something like this. Sunday is the first day I skip taking prozac. By late in the day, I experience increasing depression. Then on Monday, I experience significant anxiety, as well as continuing depression. However, shortly after this, things being to improve. Usually in the evening – generally on Monday evening or Tuesday evening – I begin to feel much better. The next day (i.e. either Tuesday or Wednesday), I feel like my "old self". This deteriorates some the following day. By Thursday, things are significantly worse again. Taking the fluoxetine on Friday then again results in moderate anxiety. Which lifts and provides a better (sometimes good) day on Saturday.

Still, even with the discontinuation process, my overall average mental state seems to be about the same. While the low periods are still bad, the good periods, if anything, are getting better and lasting slightly longer. I know I am presently "swimming against the tide" to get off prozac, but I think it is what I need to do. I would expect things to get easier again once I have been completely off prozac for a few months.

Another value I came up with in the process of thinking about my values is "being effective at my work". Technology changes very quickly in the IT field. During just the year that I was in "survival mode" and working on remedial projects following my brain hemorrhage, lots of changes occurred in the technologies my employer was using. My company provides no training, so I realized it would be up to me to catch up. As I ran across areas where I realized my knowledge was now lacking, I made a note of them. I later prioritized these based on importance. Throughout the late summer and the fall, I systematically studied these areas at home. This is in support of two values – being effective at work now, and my long term goal of finding a new job as related to my value of enjoying my work.

By late summer, work had improved somewhat. As I got better at the technologies I was using, doing my job was easier and more fun. In addition, as I learned new things, I started getting assigned to more interesting tasks. Sometimes work was even somewhat fun, particularly on my "up" days. As my boss would describe the requirements of a project, he would ask if I was comfortable working with a particular technology. "Easy day!", I would sometimes say (an allusion to the Seal Fit training). And I would get a big sense of accomplishment as I resolved the issues at hand, using technology I had just learned. Of course, not every day was like that. I still got pulled into fire-fighting from time to time, and still spent much time dealing with inadequate resources. That would kill any fun I was having on a "up" day, and could even lead me almost to the point of panic when I was in a low mental state. But it sure was an improvement from the constant "survival mode" of a year earlier.

WHAT I HAVE LEARNED

So what exactly happened? Why did I have such severe mental issues after my brain aneurysm, particularly when I had practically no mental symptoms when I initially returned home from the hospital? Were all the issues psychological? Were they the result of the brain trauma itself? I've spent literally hundreds of hours thinking about things like this over the past year and a half. More importantly, what have I learned and how have I grown from my experience?

When I first began to develop mental symptoms in late June 2013, I assumed they were all psychological. After all, I've had significant issues with anxiety, and depression, at various times in my life dating all the way back to early childhood. My assumption was that it was just the stress caused by my brain aneurysm and its subsequent aftermath that was causing any issues I was having. And in fact, that may be true to some extent. However, reading at brain aneurysm support forums (which I did just before my second surgery in April 2014) does in fact show that many people, without a previous history of psychological issues, experience similar symptoms following a brain aneurysm or other type of stroke. Similar symptoms are often experienced by those suffering traumatic brain injury (from sports or war injuries, for example).

In my case, I do believe that physical effects from the brain trauma itself did play a significant role. However, they were far from the only factor. The more in balance one's life is, the better they are able to handle stressful events. Someone whose life is out of balance may do well as long as things are going smoothly, but collapse mentally when a big storm in life hits. Such a pattern is evident in workaholics who experience a heart attack[22]. It is obvious to me that my life was way out of balance at the time I experienced my brain aneurysm. Being out of balance did not cause the aneurysm, but it did severely interfere with my ability to deal with its aftermath.

One indication of a balanced life would seem to me to be being comfortable doing a wide variety of things. The person with a balanced life can get enjoyment from work, but they would also know when to relax. They would enjoy spending time with family, as well as with friends. They would have hobbies that allow for a change from work and for relaxation. In my case, I was the exact opposite of this. I was like the classic workaholic, who works late into the night and on weekends. Such a person has no desire to be with family or friends. The

---

[22] See Eliot, Robert and Breo, Dennis in Bibliography.

only thing that matters to them is work. They will argue that they love their work, and that it is not at all stressful to them. But being out of balance like this is inherently stressful, and can lead to physical problems including a heart attack.

I was definitely this workaholic. But not with my job. At my job, I worked 40 hours a week. Overtime was fairly rare. Indeed, a big part of the reason I had chosen to stay with my current employer, despite some growing problems there, was that there was minimal overtime and thus more time to pursue hobbies. My workaholism concerned my hobbies. If I worked 40 hours each week on the job, I no doubt worked at least another 40 learning things. I might spend dozens of hours during a particular week working on a climate simulation program or a program to decode a particular type of radio signal. I studied physics, including such complicated topics as relativity and quantum theory. I spent countless hours studying for an engineering exam that would show that I still knew how do do engineering, two and a half decades after receiving my engineering degree.

There was no time for relaxation, much less any social activities. Holidays, such at the Thanksgiving and Christmas season, were a chance for me to tie up loose ends on my projects, and book more time learning. Others at work and on Facebook would describe how they had spent their Thanksgiving holiday visiting relatives. What I gave thanks for was that I no longer had to "waste" time in this way. Since I had no family, I was free to do exactly what I wanted over the holidays. Not that there is anything wrong with hobbies per se. But having all my eggs in one basket with a very narrow pattern of interests was not good. I didn't realize how much I was burning myself out. Like the workaholic who stays at work 16 hours a day, I would have denied that such a lifestyle was stressful.

Often, a workaholic is using work as an escape. For example, they may be working so many hours to "get away from" problems at home – perhaps issues with their marriage or to be away from an errant son or daughter. Was I running from something? And if so, what? Perhaps one thing I was running from was a realization of my limited time on earth and my mortality. Though I had always enjoyed working on technical stuff, it seemed that in the years leading up to my brain aneurysm that I had really thrown myself into them more. Every time I heard a reminder of how limited time is, I would use this as a motivation to work harder at the things that were important to me. For example, in 2012, my doctor said that, statistically, someone of my age had nearly a 30% risk of a cardiac event in the next ten years. "Okay, so I have a one in three chance of having a heart attack within ten years! Then there's no time to waste. Next year, I will work remotely and concentrate on storm chasing.", I told myself. When a co-worker had a close relative die unexpectedly, my only comment to him was something like "See, life is short! No time to waste! You've got to do what is important to you today!"

Another thing I was running from was my own negativity and rumination. Throughout my life, I've always been bothered by any problem I was not in control of. As an adolescent and young adult, the state of the world bothered me. Since there was little I could do about it, I learned to distract myself by concentrating on things that I could control. As my father began experiencing significant health issues with arthritis beginning around 2012, I would find myself getting depressed if I thought about him. So I practiced distracting myself with other interests.

My stress from always being so busy also took a toll on my temper. Like the classical "Type A Personality", anything that was a source of delay infuriated me. A traffic delay coming home from work? I would scream profanities, and would remain on-edge for most of the evening as a result of the irritation. A haircut? I don't have time for that! In 2012, I once had to wait a half hour for a haircut, despite having made an appointment. Right then and there, I resolved to get around that problem in the future. I bought my own "self-haircut" kit, and had not been back to the barber since. And heaven forbid if I did actually have to work a few hours overtime for a work issue. I would be upset for days afterwards. And if the neighbor's dog was barking while I was trying to solve a programming issue at home? Well, you get the idea.

Like relaxation, social life was non-existent for me. Sure, I would say hi to co-workers, and we might even discuss work tasks. But we never talked about personal things, and I never spent time with any friends outside of work. Church? Yes, I did teach Sunday School. I felt it was important, and I wanted to help. But did I "get into" it? I had not for several years. It was just another task to be done, before I could get home to work on things that I enjoyed more. I knew practically none of the parents of my kids personally, and even among the kids there were many names I hadn't learned. I didn't feel lonely or socially isolated. I did get to interact with people. It was only on a technical level, but I was to busy to notice that being an issue. Everyone, both at church and at work, knew I had few social skills, but that was okay with them. I made up for it and earned respect with all my knowledge. I was the one to go to if someone had an obscure science or technical question.

Following my brain aneurysm, my unbalanced life came crashing down. My whole life was technical interests, but now I could no longer concentrate well enough to pursue these due to anxiety an depression. I had practically no social support. That was a logical consequence of my lack of previous social involvement. The only way I knew how to relate to people was as a problem-solver. No longer doing cutting-edge technical things, I no longer had things to talk about with co-workers or on forums. Body stress, caused by years of "running on adrenaline", did not magically go away just because I was now doing less. In fact, it got worse, because I now had the stress of my brain aneurysm and its complications, as well as now having to face the problems I had been avoiding with all my previous distractions.

Being an engineer, I've always taken a very practical approach to problem solving. If x is causing a problem, then do y to fix the problem. If negative thoughts are causing me to feel depressed, then get rid of the thoughts. But as I learned from ACT[23], engineering techniques that work with the "external world" do not work with the internal world of the mind. The mind is not a passive system, like the world "out there". It has feedback mechanisms that often produce the opposite of the effects intended when attempting control. Trying to suppress negative thoughts only causes them to get stronger. Running away from office mates who are talking about distressing topics, or avoiding places that remind one of negative things, only serves to increase the anxiety associated with these situations in the future. Distracting myself from developing problems at work by taking refuge in my hobbies at home only allows the work problems to continue to grow. Taking a tranquilizer for sleep or to reduce anxiety only results in worse insomnia and anxiety as the body quickly habituates to its effects.

In relation to not trying to control or "run from" thoughts as described above, another big issue I faced following my brain aneurysm was a lack of expressing myself. I tried to gloss over anything that was wrong. At work, many things were wrong. Management resources were so scarce that project management was woefully lacking. I found myself frequently without the

---

[23] See Bibliography entry for Hayes and Wilson.

information I needed to work effectively. Development environments were inadequate, frequently inoperable, or not available at all. But I didn't feel "qualified" to really object much. What did I know? What right did I have to complain? My boss had "forgiven" me three weeks of sick time. He was keeping me on easier projects (even if they were quite tedious). Some of my co-workers were putting in 60 hour weeks to meet client deadlines. So shouldn't I be thankful for what I had? Likewise with the Christian Care and Support class at church. Many people at church had prayed for my survival during my hospitalization. And it had worked – I had indeed survived. And many people from church had helped me during my recovery. And I still needed their help with transportation for medical procedures. What right did I have to complain when it seemed like their over-zealousness was (in some cases) actually making things worse for their care receivers?

Prior to my brain aneurysm, I would have faced such problems head on. I would have frequently expressed my concerns at work, insisting that my boss make time to listen. I would have found another job had these concerns not been addressed. And I would never have been willing to get involved in something as time-consuming as Christian Care and Support. But I was too scared to "make waves" given all the issues I was facing.

I also have to consider the role that taking fluoxetine (prozac) for nearly 13 years had on my balance and psychological heartiness. It is my opinion, based on research I have done, that fluoxetine served as something that enabled me to escape from issues I should have been facing over those 13 years. Sure, I never experienced any significant anxiety or depression for nearly 12 of those 13 years. But I think what it allowed me to do is sweep problems under the rug. There were things in my life I should have been addressing. These issues only got worse the longer I waited to address them.

I know this will be controversial, because the thinking of psychiatrists presently is that people who have a past history of multiple depressive episodes should remain on antidepressants for life. But read some books on this[24], or do your own research on the internet. Why have depression and anxiety increased so much in recent years? If antidepressants work so well, wouldn't we expect to see less depression over time, not orders of magnitude more? Like a tranquilizer, I think an antidepressant can serve a purpose in the short term. When I had my thyroid issues back in 1990, I was so anxious and depressed that I couldn't even read. At that point, taking an antidepressant made sense. But I think that taking an antidepressant (or a tranquilizer for that matter) should be thought of in the same way as getting a loan. If you have a disaster in your life, a loan can help you get back on your feet. On the other hand, getting a "loan" all the time by constantly charging things to one's credit card can cause big problems with debt. To me, the

---

[24] See Whitaker, Robert in Bibliography.

present emphasis on antidepressants (with now one in 9 adults taking one at any given time[25]) is way misguided. I certainly don't blame "prozac poop out" for all or even most of the problems that I experienced following my brain aneurysm. But I do think that it blinded me to problems that I should have been addressing all along.

[25] "Astounding Increase in Antidepressant Use by Americans", Harvard Health Publications, http://www.health.harvard. edu/blog/astounding-increase-in-antidepressant-use-by-americans-201110203624.

BIBLIOGRAPHY

Benson, Herbert, M.D. The Relaxation Response. Avon Books 1976.
Describes how to perform generic meditation techniques for stress reduction.

Bregin, Peter R., M.D. And Cohen, David, Ph.D. Your Drug May Be Your Problem: How and Why to Stop Taking Psychiatric Medications. Perseus Books 2007.
Discusses harmful effects of benzodiazepines, antidepressants, and other psychiatric drugs. Provides guidelines and what to expect when getting off these drugs.

Burns, David D. The Feeling Good Handbook. Penguin Group 1989.
Probably the best book out there on self-help cognitive therapy to deal with thought distortions present in anxiety and depression.

Carnegie, Dale. <u>How to Stop Worrying and Stop Living</u>. Simon and Schuster 1984.
One of the original self-help books, first published in the 1940s. Dated, but still some very good techniques for handling worry and anxiety.

Divine, Mark. <u>The Way of the Seal</u>. Readers Digest Books 2013.
The chapter on mental toughness is helpful in dealing with adversity. Also contains practical information on dealing with problems in general.

Duncan, Les. <u>Brain Storms: Surviving Catastrophic Illness</u>. Tate Publishing 2008.
Contains practical information about dealing handling life circumstances following a stroke or other serious illness.

Dyer, Wayne. <u>Excuses Begone!: How to Change Lifelong, Self-Defeating Thinking Habits</u>. Hay House 2009.
Very logical approach to dealing with excuses and bad mental habits that prevent one from moving forward in life.

Dyer, Wayne. <u>The Power of Intention</u>. Hay House 2004.
Discusses how thoughts affect your reality and life circumstances and how to remain balanced.

Eliot, Robert S., M.D., and Breo, Dennis L. Is It Worth Dying For?. Bantam Books 1984.
This book is specifically about how to change lifestyle habits that lead to heart attack. But it is also quite applicable to anyone living an unbalanced life in general.

Graveline, Duane, M.D. The Statin Damage Crisis. Duane Graveline MD MPH 2012.
Discusses negative effects of statin (cholesterol lowering) drugs.

Harris, Russ. The Happiness Trap: How to Stop Struggling and Start Living. Trumpeter Books 2008.
Very readable and practical information on overcoming anxiety and depression using self-help Acceptance and Commitment Therapy.

Hart, Dr. Archibald D. The Anxiety Cure: You Can Find Emotional Tranquility and Wholeness. Thomas Nelson Publishers 1999.
Discusses how misuse of the body's adrenal system leads to anxiety. Contains practical tips for getting life back in balance. Note that the author is a minister and not a medical doctor, but he has practical advice nonetheless.

Hart, Dr. Archibald D. Thrilled to Death: How the Endless Pursuit of Pleasure is Leaving Us Numb. Thomas Nelson Publishers 2007.
Discusses how addiction to pleasure in our society is leading to burnout. Note that the author is a minister

and not a medical doctor, but he has practical advice nonetheless.

Hayes, Steven C., Strosahl, Kirk D., Wilson, Kelly G. <u>Acceptance and Commitment Therapy</u>. Guilford Press 2012.
This is an academic book, meant for therapists, that discusses the logic behind various ACT techniques and how to apply them. Probably not the best book for a lay person, but good for someone with an interest in psychology and how things work. If you have an ACT therapist available where you live, they are your best option. But since there are no ACT therapists available to me I used this book to learn how to work on myself.

Hobson-Dupont, Jack. <u>The Benzo Book: Getting Safely Off Tranqualizers</u>. Lulu Publishers 2012.
Discusses long-term adverse effects of benzodiazepines, how to get off of them, and what to expect during withdrawal.

Jacobs, Gregg D., PH.D. <u>Say Good Night to Insomnia</u>. Henry Holt and Company 1998.
Practical techniques for overcoming insomnia through sleep hygiene.

Kabat-Zinn, Jon. <u>Full Catastrophe Living</u>. Bantom Books 2013.
Practical guide on quieting an overactive mind and keeping thoughts in the present.

Mercer, E. Robert. <u>Worse than Heroin: The World's Most Difficult Addiction Problem</u>. 2008.
One person's story of how he became addicted to benzodiazepines despite following his doctor's medication orders exactly. Discusses his struggle to get off benzodiazepines. His story is helpful during benzo withdrawal to realize that other people have gone through worse and still recovered to live a normal life.

Pattakos, Alex PH.D. <u>Prisoners of Our Thoughts</u>. Berret-Koehler Publishers 2010.
Describes how Victor Frankl was able to find life meaning and remain upbeat despite the suffering caused by being a prisoner in a Nazi concentration camp in World War II. Discusses his techniques and how we can apply them to our adversities.

Peale, Norman Vincent. <u>The Power of Positive Thinking</u>. Prentice Hall 1956.
Perhaps the most famous religious inspirational book of all time, written by a minister. This is a very inspiring and comforting book to read during difficult times. Concentrating on the positive is indeed helpful. However, it should not be at the expense of denying or trying to push the negative out of one's mind. I found that attempting to push negative thoughts away only makes them far worse in the long run. It is important to think positively, but also to honestly acknowledge and address the negative.

Peck, M. Scott, M.D. **The Road Less Traveled**. Simon and Schuster 1978.
The author is a Christian, but he also discusses toxic effects of well-meaning religious figures on himself and his patients and how to overcome these. Helpful in striking a balance between faith and reason.

Stephen, Joseph, PhD. **What Doesn't Kill Us: The New Psychology of Posttraumatic Growth**. Perseus Books 2011.
Discusses the history, causes and symptoms of PTSD, and contains practical techniques for dealing with it.

Stephens, Sasha. **The Effortless Sleep Method: The Incredible New Cure for Insomnia and Chronic Sleep Problems**. 2010.
Practical techniques for overcoming insomnia through sleep hygiene.

Whitaker, Robert. **Anatomy of An Epidemic: Magic Bullets, Psychiatric Drugs, and the Astonishing Rise of Mental Illness in America**. Broadway Books 2011.
Very well researched and documented information on how psychiatric drugs can cause a severe worsening of psychological problems that they attempt to treat in the long term.